American
GRIT

American GRIT

From a Japanese American Concentration Camp Rises an American War Hero

JOHN SUZUKI

JohnSuzuki.com

Copyright © 2023 by John Suzuki

All rights reserved. No part of this book may be reproduced, distributed, or transmitted in any form or by any means, including photocopying, recording, or other electronic or mechanical methods, without the prior written permission of the author, except in the case of brief quotations embodied in critical reviews and certain other noncommercial uses permitted by copyright law.

First edition published 2023

Published by Finding Better Press
JohnSuzuki.com

ISBN (hardcover): 979-8-9883706-2-8
ISBN (paperback): 979-8-9883706-0-4
ISBN (ebook): 979-8-9883706-1-1

Book design and production by www.AuthorSuccess.com

Printed in the United States of America

Dedicated to the men, women, and children imprisoned in the Japanese American concentration camps of World War II, the 442nd Regimental Combat Team, 100th Battalion, Military Intelligence Service, and all of the men and women who have served in the United States Armed Forces.

May our future be one of love and remembrance.

Contents

Foreword by Kimotomo "Kim" Muromoto   ix
Introduction   1

1: Fear and Hysteria   5
2: When American Babies were Incarcerated   13
3: Beauty and the Flirt   21
4: Home in an American Concentration Camp   31
5: For the Sake of the Children   44
6: Save the Texans   64
7: More Lost than Saved   76
8: Incarcerated Again   91
9: The Impossible Mission   95
10: Heroes Not Welcome   114
11: His Final Battle   126
12: Valor Undefeated   140

Epilogue: American Grit   146
Acknowledgements   170
Resources   172
Appendix A: A Truly Great Nation   174
Thank You   182

Foreword

BY KIMOTOMO "KIM" MUROMOTO

I celebrated my 101st birthday on January 10, 2024 and I still remember February 19, 1942 like it was yesterday when President Roosevelt signed Executive Order 9066. My entire family was evicted from our farm in Bellevue, Washington, and then evacuated by the United States Army from the West Coast to the Minidoka concentration camp in Idaho.

My parents were so angry at Japan for attacking America and so fearful and confused for our future. But nothing could prepare us for the hardship and anguish of the camps and the utter fear we faced as our own country, the United States of America, declared American citizens of Japanese ancestry to be enemies of America. Over 120,000 of us were incarcerated in concentration camps in areas of America not meant for human life. And then came the opportunity for young men like me to be released from the camps by going to war against America's enemies, as our families remained imprisoned by the U.S. Army.

Being part of the 442nd Regimental Combat Team was one of the greatest honors of my life. We were brothers fighting not only for America, but for a better life against terrible discrimination in America. I fought side-by-side with Shiro "Kash" Kashino and George Morihiro in the Battle of the Gothic Line and was lucky to have survived the war. As I had forgotten much about my World War II experiences over so many years, reading this book brought back many tragic memories of the camps and my wartime experiences, and also reminded me of what we fought for and accomplished before, during, and after World War II.

All of us who were incarcerated and suffered the indignity of having been rounded up and thrown into a God-forsaken concentration camp wish for our experiences to never be forgotten. And of the Nisei men of the 100th Battalion, 442nd Regimental Combat Team, and the Military Intelligence Service, our hope is that our contributions in winning the war and proving our loyalty to make life better for future generations of Americans will also be remembered. It is especially in this spirit of keeping our memory alive that I am grateful for this book.

God bless you, and may God bless America.

Kimitomo "Kim" Muromoto
442nd Regimental Combat Team, 1944-1945

January 10, 1923 – June 17, 2024

Kimitomo "Kim" Muromoto passed away peacefully shortly before this edition of *American Grit* went to press. He was an American hero.

Mr. Muromoto, thank you for your service to America and for making the world better for all of us.

Introduction

American Grit is one of the greatest love stories ever lived – of country, family, and our future—during a time when American citizens were unjustly persecuted, evicted from the West Coast, and incarcerated in concentration camps across America during World War II. Many lost their homes, farms, businesses, and life savings, and nobody knew what their future held, or even if they had one. Many became victims of their circumstances. Some committed suicide. Their crime: they *looked* like the Japanese enemy.

Then out of the ashes rose young men who refused to blame others for their circumstances and refused to succumb to victimhood. Instead they chose to take control of their lives and fight to prove their loyalty to America. They fought to build a better life for future generations, volunteered to fight America's enemies, and became part of the most decorated fighting unit in the history of the United States for its size and duration. Instead of being victims of their lives, they became champions of their lives, and this is their story.

After Japan bombed Pearl Harbor on December 7, 1941, launching the United States into World War II, President Franklin Delano Roosevelt signed Executive Order 9066, which gave the United States Army complete power to imprison Japanese American citizens in concentration camps scattered across the deserts and swamps of America for no other reason than their heritage.

It was the summer of 2008 when I joined a pilgrimage to one of the ten former United States concentration camps—also referred to as "internment" and "relocation" camps—built to imprison over 122,000 people of Japanese ancestry during World War II, two-thirds of whom were American citizens, and about 50,000 were children and babies. It was called Minidoka and located outside of Twin Falls, Idaho, and housed over 13,000 inmates. When I boarded the bus for the twelve-hour drive to Minidoka, I learned that everyone on the trip had some connection to Minidoka through their own experiences, or someone in their family having been imprisoned there. When I was asked why I was going, I told the group that while I am a third-generation Japanese American myself with an inherent interest in the Japanese American experiences of World War II, I really had no idea why I was going since neither my parents nor anyone in my extended family were interned in Minidoka. I went on to say that I somehow knew I would know why I was there by the time I boarded the bus coming home.

While the land around what was once Minidoka is now fertile farmland, I imagined what it was like during World War II when it was nothing but barren desert and tumbleweeds. It was truly an unforgiving land unsuitable for normal human living, with temperatures reaching over 100°F in the summer and well below freezing in the winter. But as miserable as life was in Minidoka, what hit me the hardest was the Honor Roll that was being renewed. It was a billboard

Minidoka Honor Roll. Photo courtesy of Densho

that listed the names of the Japanese American men who *volunteered* from the Minidoka internment camp to fight for the United States Army; the same Army that imprisoned them and their families in Minidoka. This was a kind of heroism unmatched by anything I had ever heard of, and suddenly the reason for my being there was crystal clear; this was a story that had to be shared.

I immediately got to work writing a screenplay, believing that the fastest way to the American psyche was through a major motion picture, and decided that the perfect story would be about a Japanese American who was imprisoned at Minidoka, fought in two of the most epic battles of World War II, and became an American war hero. But the problem was that I didn't know if such a man existed. After months of research, I finally found the man whose experience matched what I was looking for. His name was Shiro Kashino, and I was terribly disappointed when I learned that he had passed away eleven years earlier in 1997.

Undeterred, I reached out to his widow via registered letters, and the day she called me and agreed to collaborate with me on this project was one of the most exciting days of my life. Her name was Louise Kashino and we worked together on this project for eleven years, during which time we became good friends, and I switched gears from writing a screenplay to writing this book. And then my heart broke on August 20, 2019, when Louise passed away. She was an amazing woman, in a lot of ways even more amazing than her late husband.

Before she died, Louise asked her daughter, Debbie Kashino, to continue our collaboration to complete this project. Louise felt this book—and hopefully a future movie—would serve as a cautionary tale of how the panic and fear of war led to the indiscriminate targeting of a race, along with telling the tale of the remarkable journey of an American hero. In her words as a proud and grateful American, "May the world never forget what over 122,000 victims of the American concentration camps went through, and the heroism of Japanese

Americans in World War II." This is why I wrote this book; to help fulfill the one common wish of the many folks I interviewed. That their experiences in the camps and at war be shared with the world and never be forgotten.

My journey in writing this book has been one of a series of incredible miracles that became a labor of love and a personal promise to complete (Please see the Epilogue "My American Grit Story"). It is a journey of meeting amazing people whose stories have changed my life and perspectives on how it is truly our duty—yours and mine—to understand and learn from the past to shape our future for generations to come, and to do our part to keep the bad experiences of days gone by from ever being repeated.

Louise mentioned that Shiro was a humble man who would never have allowed a book like this to be written about him. I told her that since she was giving me permission, I would write it with the hope that when I finally meet him in heaven, he will shake my hand with a hearty smile and not yell at me. On the other hand, if he yells at me and then shakes my hand with a hearty smile, I'll be happy with that too.

To Shiro, Louise, Debbie, and the Kashino family, thank you for your story, and thank you for giving me the honor of sharing it with the world. My hope and prayer are that Shiro and Louise are looking down from the heavens and happy with this work. I love you.

1

Fear and Hysteria

His legs buckled and his face went flush. Reading the notice posted on the street corner outside of his apartment building, he could not believe his eyes. Taking off his glasses, he wiped them off and reread it. Suddenly he was faced with an official notice instructing him and all who shared his ancestry to report for evacuation. Although he had read about Nazi Germany rounding up Jews and confiscating their property and belongings, he never thought it could possibly happen to him in his own country.

Within hours, the bulletin seemed to be posted everywhere. While they were told that they were going to camps for their own protection with "healthy food," the mandate unleashed days of panic and dread. As in Germany, all men, women, children, and the elderly were subject to evacuation and detention, and nobody was spared. The parallels were frightening, and nobody in authority could say how the situation was any different. In the days that followed, life savings were lost as family businesses were sold to profiteers for pennies on the dollar. Family treasures handed down through generations were to be left behind as families prioritized the precious few things they were permitted to take with them, as they were only allowed to bring what they could carry. Where were they going to be taken? Would they ever be allowed to come home? Some kept the hope that they would someday return, while others resigned themselves to being permanently incarcerated and never coming home. Still others feared the worst-case scenario of being taken away never to be seen again. At the stroke of a pen, his new reality included being imprisoned in some kind of prison camp in an unknown location, for no other reason than his race. All he knew was that America declared Japanese Americans on the West Coast to be "enemy aliens," despite being citizens of the United States of America.

As Shiro Kashino contemplated what was going on, he kept coming back to the same question of how things got so bad so fast. Shiro was your typical All-American, All-Star kid growing up in Seattle, Washington, but his childhood was far from typical. Born in Seattle on January 19, 1922, Shiro was a second generation Japanese American Nisei (pronounced NEE-say) whose dad, Fujinotsuke Kashino, immigrated to the United States when Japanese immigration began in the late 1800s. He came from Okayama, Japan to pursue better economic opportunities and returned to Japan in the early 1900s to marry Hatsune Ota. Shortly thereafter, they both came back to the United States to build a new life and raise a family in America.

By the 1920s, a significant Japanese community was flourishing in the United States. Mr. Kashino settled in the West Coast, where many Japanese immigrants established farms, businesses, and other ventures. He had a successful career working for an import company serving Japanese railroad workers in Montana and Wyoming. But the 1920s were also a time when many ethnicities including African Americans, Jews, Europeans, and Asians faced significant discrimination in the United States.

The Immigration Act of 1924 was a federal law that limited the number of immigrants coming to the United States from certain countries. Many lawmakers and members of the public believed that these immigrants were inferior and posed a threat to American society and wished to maintain a certain racial and ethnic makeup in the United States. The Immigration Act was a significant piece of legislation that also reflected widespread racism and nativism and contributed to the exclusion and discrimination of many minority groups, including the Japanese community.

Growing up in the 1920s, Shiro had no idea that any of this was going on. He was the youngest of six children, with his sister Fusako being eleven years older—she was the oldest of his siblings. His brother Paul was next, with his sister Fumi third, followed by his brothers Taiji and Kenzo, and then came Shiro. His mom was the backbone of the Kashino family and the main caretaker of the children. When Shiro was only three years old, tragedy struck in 1925, when his mom had to be admitted into a hospital to battle chronic illnesses. So with his dad working, caring for Shiro was left to his siblings.

During his elementary school years, Shiro's family rented a house in a mostly white area in Seattle called Leschi. Being a Japanese American child in a white neighborhood in those days came with some unique challenges, as Japan's rise as a military power and brutal expansion into Asia raised significant concerns in the United States about Japan and its global ambitions. While some parents would not let their kids play or walk home from school with him, Shiro played with anyone willing to play with him and did his best to fit in with his white neighbors and schoolmates. When an occasional racist remark would come his way, he simply shrugged it off with the childhood rhyme, "sticks and stones . . ."

In 1933, when Shiro was eleven, his mom passed away, succumbing to her years-long battle with illnesses including tuberculosis. Her death was Shiro's first jolt in realizing that she would never come home, and he would have to live the rest of his life without his mom. It was a heartbreaking time for the entire family, but since they had lived for eight years with her away from home, they had become accustomed to her absence.

The following year, tragedy struck again when Shiro's dad unexpectedly died from cancer. Shiro was only twelve and the Kashino children were suddenly left to fend for themselves. With Shiro being so young, his siblings struggled with what to do with him. While they had relatives in Japan who wanted to adopt him to carry on their family name, he had grown up in a white neighborhood and knew nothing of the Japanese culture and did not speak Japanese. There was no way Shiro was going to allow them to ship him off to Japan. And while family friends in Montana also wanted to adopt him, Shiro had no desire to go to Montana either. His siblings knew that Shiro would never willingly leave Seattle, and that if he was ever sent away or placed in an orphanage, he would run away to find his way back to them. With no other options, his older sister, Fumi, finally took him in.

Because Shiro did not want to burden Fumi or his other siblings, he did his best to fend for himself. During his teenage years, Japan's continued aggression in the Far East and their signing of an alliance with Germany led to heightened concern and animosity toward people of Japanese ancestry in the United States, especially on the West Coast. Despite what was happening on the world stage, Shiro got along well with most of the kids through sports, but being a Japanese American made him a target of racism and discrimination and he hated it. He felt it all around him and realized that if he was going to make it in this world on his own, he was going to have to learn to fight and defend himself.

Shiro felt strongly that he deserved to live in Seattle as much as anyone else, and the fact that he was of Japanese descent was not a reason for people to disrespect him. As his dad always told him, he was an American first and Japanese second. As time went on, he found it increasingly difficult to ignore the frequency of derogatory and racist remarks directed his way. While the whispers and unfriendly looks of suspicion directed at Shiro didn't bother him so much, the one thing he would not tolerate and always elicited an immediate response was being called a "Jap." It didn't matter whether the person was big, small, or even someone he knew. That one word always made him boil. The feeling was always the same; freezing in his tracks, his blood pressure spiking as he clenched his fists, his whole body ready to explode.

Shiro's breaking point happened early in high school. Somebody he didn't even know called him a "Jap" and Shiro decided that the time for his first fight was upon him. The fact that he didn't have any real fighting experience didn't matter. He knew that his anger and determination were enough to carry him to victory, but he quickly learned that there was more to winning a fight than spirit alone. After throwing what he thought were well-placed punches, Shiro found himself on the ground with a mouthful of dirt as he heard his opponent laughing as he walked away. While he didn't win that fight, he realized that his temper was not enough to keep him from eating dirt. He needed to study how to fight and learn to fight smart, especially since he had no mom to go crying home to, and he certainly did not want to be a burden on his siblings. With a few more bloody noses and black eyes, Shiro became stronger and smarter with every fight and usually figured out a way to win. As he would later say, "I got pretty good at fighting."

At the age of sixteen, Shiro moved closer to downtown Seattle and went to Garfield High School, where he got much more involved in sports and made friends of many ethnicities, including other Japanese Americans. While he wasn't a great student as far as grades were concerned, he made a reputation for himself as a gifted athlete and a fierce competitor who never backed down. Shiro was five foot ten inches and 180 pounds, which made him huge for a Japanese guy. He excelled in baseball as a third baseman and played quarterback in his junior year for Garfield High School and the All-City football team of Seattle. Despite the racism toward Japanese Americans during those days, most of Shiro's friends were white, and he tried to be friends with just about everyone. Whether they liked him or not, he was respected for his accomplishments in football and baseball.

The following year, Shiro was dealt a devastating blow when his vision got so progressively bad that he had to wear glasses to see, making him unable to play quarterback in his senior year. His request to be assigned a different position led to some discussion as to what to do with him due to his poor eyesight, as well as growing anti-Japanese sentiment and demands to have him removed from the team. Since the team knew about the hardships he had suffered growing up as a Japanese American and didn't want to lose one of their best players, they rallied around him and kept him on as a guard, a position he could play without his glasses.

As tough and hardened as he was growing up, Shiro was easy to be with and his friends said he was true to his word in always delivering on his promises. They also described him as being someone who always took care of his friends and had a kind heart for kids and animals. He always enjoyed playing with kids and would often bring

Shiro Kashino, #39 on the Garfield High football team. He played quarterback until his eyesight no longer allowed him to play quarterback, and later moved to a guard position. Photo courtesy of the Kashino family

a stray dog home to take care of for a while, giving it a little love and nourishment before sending it on its way. Because he was something of a stray himself, he was always sympathetic to those who needed help, human and non-human alike, and folks would later say that he was always happy to help others in need.

Shiro learned a lesson that he never forgot when one of the big guys in high school called him a "dirty Jap." Knowing the guy was one of the best boxers in school did not matter; Shiro knew he had to stand for what was right. As they met under the football bleachers getting ready to fight, Shiro knew that win or lose, he was going to take a beating. It was at that moment that he resolved to never give up, and that defeat was not an option. Shiro recalled over fifty years later, "Boy, that guy broke my nose and worked me over real good! ... But I was able to get behind him and I choked him out until he turned purple ... It was a really good lesson for me because I learned to fight a lot better after that."

As anti-Japanese sentiment grew, more and more stores and businesses refused to serve Japanese people as fear and suspicion grew while Japan continued its aggressive expansion across Asia, pulling the United States closer to war. Finding work was especially difficult for Japanese Americans. Racial slurs and fights became more commonplace. Shiro would walk for miles along the streets of downtown looking for a job, and finally found work at Security Market on 5th Avenue. The owner was the father of one of Shiro's teammates who was sympathetic to the plight of the Japanese American community and happy to give him a job. Unfortunately, shortly after he started working, a customer complained about having a "Jap" in the store and Shiro was reluctantly let go the next day. Clenching his fists, he controlled his frustration and thanked the store owner for the opportunity to work for him and sadly went on his way. Many years later, Shiro would describe the entire situation as "not good for us Japanese guys."

As he continued his job search, he couldn't help but wonder how he was going to make it in the world with so much discrimination and hatred against him. Every door was closed to him as he knocked on every business he came across. He was a Japanese American and nobody was willing to hire anyone who looked Japanese. It was difficult to accept, but it was his reality. After days of walking the streets and knocking on hundreds of doors, Shiro was finally welcomed and hired at Tashiro Hardware, a store owned by a Japanese American, where he worked hard to earn his keep.

Suspicion and fear of the possibility of war with Germany and Japan had hit both coasts. On the East Coast, fears of German, Italian, and Jewish spies had the government on high alert. Immigration and entry into the United States was severely cut back to anyone suspected of being sympathetic to Germany, including Jews fleeing from persecution in Europe. On the West Coast, fears of Japanese spies resulted in a curfew imposed on all people of Japanese ancestry. Other Asians were not singled out in this manner, which caused confusion since many Asians "looked alike." This led to people of other Asian ethnicities to go to great lengths to avoid being mistaken for Japanese. The Chinese community created a button that said, "I am Chinese," so they wouldn't be harassed. Knowing this, Shiro figured that if he could get a Chinese pin, nobody would be the wiser. One of his Chinese friends laughed when Shiro asked him for a pin and was happy to give him one since he knew what a scrappy guy Shiro was. While he was happy with his newfound Chinese identity which allowed him to live his life normally despite the curfew, the button also saved him from getting into trouble, as guys looking to pick a fight would look at his button and leave him alone.

2

When American Babies were Incarcerated

With World War II expanding across Europe and Asia, expectations were rising across America that the United States would eventually be pulled into the conflict. While everyone in the Japanese American community hoped that nothing bad would happen, they all feared the worst. Finally, on December 7, 1941, their worst fears came true; Japan attacked Pearl Harbor with no warning, killing over 2,400

The Japanese attack of Pearl Harbor on December 7, 1941 thrust the United States into World War II. Photo courtesy of the Library of Congress.

Americans. Cries of outrage and "Japs bomb Pearl Harbor!" were all over the news and echoed across the country. The United States immediately declared war on Japan.

"Remember Pearl Harbor!" became the American battle cry, and suddenly the eyes of fear and suspicion descended upon everyone of Japanese ancestry in Hawaii and on the West Coast. In Seattle, U.S. concerns that the Japanese would attack Boeing and the nearby naval bases kept everyone on full alert. And as anti-Japanese sentiment continued to grow, fears among the Japanese community of being attacked or brutalized by others in their communities also increased as hatred and discrimination toward anyone of Japanese ancestry spiked. Attacks against Japanese residents and their businesses became more frequent. America was suddenly at war with Japan, and fear and confusion had taken over logic and reason. Although people of Japanese ancestry had been living peacefully and responsibly in the U.S. for over fifty years, propaganda became increasingly worse resulting in mass hysteria against Japanese Americans, but the worst was still yet to come.

To protect the homeland, the U.S. government divided the West Coast into Military Zones, and on February 19, 1942, President Franklin Delano Roosevelt signed Executive Order 9066 authorizing the Secretary of War and his military commanders to evict civilians from the Military Zones. Congress then authorized those powers by passing Public Law 503, allowing the military to impose restrictions on anyone it deemed to be a threat.

The effect of Executive Order 9066 was that all persons of Japanese descent in California, Alaska, the western halves of Oregon and Washington, and

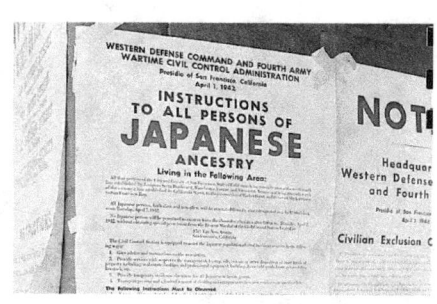

Executive Order 9066 posted outside a building. Courtesy of the National Archives and Records Administration.

southern Arizona were to be forced from their land and homes and imprisoned in American concentration camps. Over 122,000 people of Japanese ancestry were ordered to report to various detention facilities to be processed and imprisoned indefinitely, two thirds of whom were American citizens and nearly half of whom were children. There was no due process, no presumption of innocence, and no consideration of their American citizenship. The prevailing belief was that since some Japanese people might be dangerous, all of them had to be imprisoned. Nobody of Japanese ancestry in the affected areas was spared: men, women, children, babies, the elderly, and the infirmed. They were all imprisoned simply because of their heritage.

Reading Presidential Executive Order 9066 posted outside his apartment building, Shiro knew it was a moment he would never forget. He could not believe what he was reading. Fears of terrible things to come had suddenly become real, and his stomach turned. Was their fate tied to the Jews in Nazi Germany? Nobody had any way of knowing. He was angry and sad that Japan attacked the United States since it was his ancestral home, but there was no question in his mind that should it come to choosing between Japan and the United States, he would fight against Japan as an American soldier. He was born an American, and as an American he would fight.

To Shiro and tens of thousands of Japanese Americans living on the West Coast, the imposition of Executive Order 9066 was frightening and patently unfair. He was an American citizen by birth and had done nothing wrong. He was not charged with any crimes and was completely innocent. Shiro strongly believed that he was going to have to find a way to prove his worth as an American. He believed that until Japanese Americans demonstrated their loyalty, the bigotry and discrimination against them might never end.

The Japanese American residents in the military exclusion zones were informed on exactly when and where to report for their incarceration, but preparing for relocation and forced imprisonment was

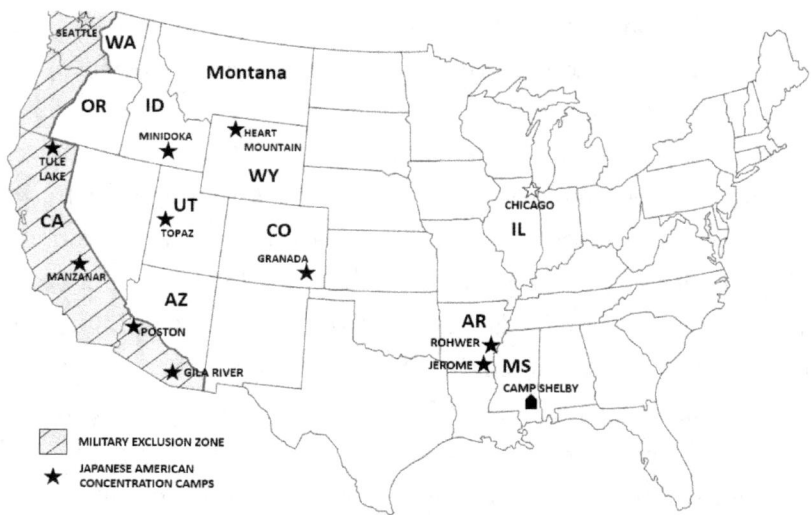

Map of the locations of the ten Japanese American concentration camps across the U.S.

traumatic for everyone. Nobody knew what was going to happen to them. Were they to be deported? Imprisoned? For how long? Nobody knew what their futures held or where they were going to be taken, so there was no way to know how to pack. Some feared that they were to be taken to the desert and shot. It was truly a terrifying time and nobody in authority gave any assurances that the worst-case scenario would not befall them.

Of all their worldly belongings, each person, including children, was only allowed to bring what they could carry. Families were given one to three weeks' notice to store or sell all their belongings. Their homes, farms, businesses, and family pets had to be left behind with friends for safekeeping or sold for pennies on the dollar to anyone willing to buy them. Finally, on March 22, 1942, the forced evacuations of Japanese Americans on the West Coast began.

During this time when people of Japanese ancestry were shunned and exploited, there were also many folks who quietly worked against the tide of fear and discrimination and supported the Japanese

Grocery store owned by Japanese Americans for sale.
Photo courtesy of Dorothea Lange, Library of Congress.

community. Reverend Emery "Andy" Andrews, the white pastor of the Japanese Baptist Church of Seattle, was one such person. Andy, as his congregation would lovingly call him, stayed true to loving and supporting his church family and never let himself be swayed by the fear and hatred of the times.

Realizing the belongings of the people being evacuated would have to be discarded, sold, or perhaps lost or stolen, Andy opened up the church gymnasium for everyone in the Japanese community, Christians and non-Christians alike, to store their most valued belongings until they returned. Days before Japanese residents left their homes to be evacuated, they came to the gymnasium and dropped off their things, entrusting Andy for their safekeeping until their return.

As a twenty-year-old, Shiro didn't have much in terms of material belongings, but ended up selling everything he couldn't take, including his car and furniture. He only kept what he could carry, including the official notice of when he had to report to the bus that would take him away. On the night before he was to report, Shiro got together with a bunch of his friends to "paint the town." Wanting to make the most of their last night of freedom, they ordered a couple of rounds of drinks and got increasingly rowdy as the evening went on. Anyone who called Shiro a "Jap" that night got a mouthful of knuckles. He woke up a little sore in the morning but didn't remember much about the previous evening. His buddies told him that a bunch of guys from the night before probably wouldn't be calling them "Japs" again.

Shiro arrived at the specific time and location as instructed to catch the bus that took him to the Puyallup Fairgrounds (pronounced Pew-AH-lupp), twenty miles south of Seattle. Everyone had a name tag attached to their shirt, as if they were a piece of luggage. While the humiliation was hard to stomach, every person and every bag had to be accounted for, and the use of identification tags was the best solution the U.S. Army could think of at the time. Shiro carried two duffle bags containing everything he owned. As the men, women, children, and old people struggled to carry their suitcases and bulging bags filled with their worldly belongings, he did what he could to help. The bus was packed with Japanese people of all ages, from infants to the elderly, with everyone desperate to know their fate after having had their lives destroyed and upended by Executive Order 9066. Shiro, like everyone else, had no idea what awaited him.

As they approached the Puyallup Fairgrounds, a happy and welcoming place during better times, Shiro was shocked to see that everything festive had been stripped away, and the fairgrounds converted into a prison camp surrounded by tall, barbed wire fences and armed guards with rifles. Stepping off the bus, he looked around to get his bearings. Through the cold, wet, and mud, Shiro could hardly comprehend the misery he was witnessing. American soldiers stood over them as their jailers. The bewildered and fearful looks on everyone's faces, as they held hands and huddled with their loved ones, betrayed their hopes that their worries and fears would not come to pass. It was an epic nightmare for every man, woman, and child as

Members of a Japanese American family await an evacuation bus to transport them to a military detention center. Photo courtesy of the Dorothea Lange Collection.

they were suddenly thrust into prison life, their freedom as Americans taken from them for no other reason than their race.

It was called "Camp Harmony," but there was nothing harmonious about it. It was cold, crowded, and stunk of farm animals. American soldiers with rifles and bayonets shouted orders at arriving families. Children cried as a sea of confused humanity jockeyed around trying to figure out what they were to do next and where to go. The entire scene was surreal; something Shiro never imagined could happen to him in his own country. Each person and family were assigned living quarters according to the name tags tied to their clothes. Finding their quarters in the sprawling prison camp was their first challenge. Of equal if not higher priority was finding food and a bathroom. It was a scene of madness that would be replayed across thirteen designated "assembly centers" where Japanese Americans were detained for their eventual incarceration in one of ten internment camps being built in some of the most uninhabitable places across the country. Looking around, Shiro finally realized his fate; he was now a prisoner of war in his own country, the United States of America.

3

Beauty and the Flirt

Louise Tsuboi was attending her senior year of high school at Broadway High in Seattle when the Japanese unleashed hell on Pearl Harbor. Gathered around the radio with her family on December 7, 1941, Louise was horrified to learn that Japan launched a surprise attack on the United States. It was an especially upsetting day for her parents, who had spent nearly three decades building an honorable life in America. They were furious and dismayed that Japan attacked Pearl Harbor and knew that their heritage country going to war with the United States would be trouble for them.

Louise's dad immigrated to the United States in 1913 and worked any job he could find: lumber, fishing, or janitorial work. Her mom came to America in 1917. A strong and determined woman, she immigrated on her own to start a new life for herself, which was very unusual for Japanese women in those days. After meeting each other, they traveled back to Japan to get married, and returned to the United States in 1919 to pursue their American dream. Eventually, Mr. Tsuboi became a food peddler, selling fruits and vegetables from the back of a truck.

The Tsubois were a family of eight. In order, Hideko was the oldest, followed by Frank, Louise, Henry, Roy, and Esther. They were all roughly two years apart and were raised with traditional Japanese values of respect, honesty, minding your parents, diligence, hard work, and most of all, not bringing shame to the family. They were also taught to "never rock the boat" and always be obedient. Her mom was an incredibly strong and business-savvy woman who kept the family close and always made sure her children honored and lived the values they were taught.

In 1934, when Louise was eight years old, the Tsubois bought a grocery store called Minor Grocery just north of downtown Seattle in what was then the Cascade area. Louise spent most of her childhood living behind the grocery store with her family. Over the next eight years, the Tsubois built a full-fledged store with produce from local farmers, coffee beans, loose-leaf tea, milk, cottage cheese, a wide variety of groceries, and fish brought in from the bay each morning. Louise's dad had always been generous, quietly extending credit when customers needed it. During the Great Depression, many people had come to use the grocer as a kind of bank that would cover them until they got their next paycheck. Mr. Tsuboi's generosity prevented many people from going hungry, and he never discriminated on the basis of skin color, since the Great Depression hit everyone indiscriminately.

Louise and her sisters spent their afternoons after school in the store, helping out and learning the business. As Louise would later say, "When you own a business, it owns you. Sometimes you love it, sometimes you hate it, but it's totally part of the family." After having spent endless hours and energy building their store and reinvesting their profits back into state-of-the-art equipment and supplies, the news of Pearl Harbor brought great concern for what was to happen to them.

Rumors of incarcerating Japanese residents who were non-American citizens were becoming widespread, and since Mr. and Mrs. Tsuboi were not American citizens, it suddenly dawned on them that they could be arrested and put in prison at any time. What was the family to do? Since nobody imagined American children would be incarcerated, they planned for Frank and Louise to run the store in their parents' absence. Louise had grown up helping to run the store and was confident that with good planning and guidance from her parents, she and Frank could take care of it for as long as they had to. But all their meticulous planning went out the window when Executive Order 9066 was announced.

Louise could not believe what she was reading. Like everyone who read the notice, she was stunned and bewildered to learn that all people of Japanese heritage, including American citizens, were to be taken away and incarcerated. No exceptions. The entire Tsuboi family was to be imprisoned, and nobody would be allowed to stay home and mind their businesses or belongings. It was a nightmare of epic proportions that no one could have ever expected or prepared for. The idea that they could only bring what they could carry presented two daunting challenges; deciding what to bring, and what to do with what they couldn't. Nobody knew where they were going or for how long, so to think that they had to carry everything they needed to survive and treasured was absurd, and yet they had no choice. All they could take were the bare necessities of life.

Mr. Tsuboi tried desperately to find someone to buy his store at a fair price, but the Japanese community fell victim to the circumstances and unscrupulous profiteers. He sold his store at the last minute, including all equipment, appliances, and entire inventory for $2,000, which amounted to mere pennies on the dollar. Most upsetting was having to sell his car, his pride and joy which he had recently purchased, for a pittance of $200. It was truly heartbreaking.

After finally deciding on what they would take with them, they boxed up everything else for storage. One of their neighbors was kind enough to store everything for them in one of his boarding houses and take care of their belongings until they returned. As she tearfully packed her party clothes, school awards, precious books, and all her life's treasures, Louise could only hope and pray that she could someday reclaim them. But the most painful part of her experience was realizing that everything her parents earned and worked so hard for over so many years was evaporating, virtually into thin air. It was beyond heartbreaking. The Tsubois moved their furniture, home appliances, and all their belongings into the neighbor's boarding house, greatly appreciating his kindness and hospitality.

On May 14, 1942, Louise and her family abandoned their home and store and were taken away from the life they loved and worked so hard for. Like so many other Japanese American families, the Tsubois packed all that they could, but their home and store were gone. Louise would later recall when her parents walked around their beloved store in a daze and in disbelief, hardly able to believe that their nightmare was real. As they prepared to leave their home, their spirit seemed to shift. It was as if they were snapping themselves into their new reality; from sadness and fear to strength and determination. While nobody knew what was to become of them, they were resolved in doing their damnedest to keep their family safe and together.

It was a cold, dark day as they left the key under the mat for the new owner. The Tsubois stood strong and held their heads high as they walked away dressed in their Sunday best. As angry and indignant as they were about what was happening to them, Mr. and Mrs. Tsuboi held their emotions intact. While they thought that someone from their neighborhood would show up and drive them to the bus stop where they were ordered to report, their neighbors turned their backs on them, which felt like salt poured on already deep wounds. For nearly a decade they had served the community, supported their families, and lent them money. And now, in their time of their greatest need, Louise was heartbroken to see that nobody who she thought were their friends seemed to care. Grimly, they held their composure and took two cabs to 14th and Jefferson, clinging to what amounted to the entirety of their worldly possessions.

As Louise and her family boarded the bus to a completely unknown future, she took a seat next to her mother. Looking out the window, she quietly cried to herself, knowing that she may never see Seattle again.

Looking around, Louise was surprised by how silent and obedient everyone was as they did exactly as they were told and never made waves. Louise heard some folks say the Japanese phrase "*Shikata ga nai*" (loosely translated, "there's nothing you can do about it so be quiet and stay strong"), which was exactly what she did. Everyone seemed lost in their own thoughts about what was happening to them, helpless and fearful of what their future held.

Arriving at Camp Harmony, they were met with the grim sight of the Puyallup Fairgrounds having been converted into a giant military prison housing over 10,000 inmates of Japanese descent. The whole experience was nothing short of surreal. As she stepped off the bus, Louise saw barbed wire fences and guard towers with large spotlights and knew in an instant that Camp Harmony was not for their protection, but for their detention and imprisonment. Each new inhabitant knew their freedom was lost as they waved at non-Japanese friends outside the barbed wire fencing, armed soldiers watching over them. The rain added to the misery, making everything cold and muddy. As they reported into camp, Louise and her family were given the location of their living quarters and burlap bags to fill with straw. She and Mrs. Tsuboi held their emotions in check as they picked up the ticking and stuffed the bags that would serve as their mattresses for the next few months.

The Tsubois were assigned to a tar paper-covered barrack, which reminded Louise of a storage shack they had behind the store. Never one to complain (*Shikata ga nai*), Mrs. Tsuboi quietly and resolutely started making the beds for her family. There was a cot for each of them, with a pile of scratchy woolen blankets that were entirely insufficient against the piercing cold. Mr. Tsuboi laid the burlap bags on each cot. With gaps in the walls made of lumber all around them, the uninsulated barrack provided little protection from the outside elements and felt much like they were sleeping outside. On the inside, every sound and conversation could be heard, including those that were meant to be private. But soon the sad truth became obvious that Louise and her family were actually some of the lucky ones. Where the Tsubois were assigned to a new barrack of wood and tarpaper, many families were assigned to stay in what were animal stalls just days before that reeked of animal feces, causing many to vomit as they inhaled the stench. Eventually, the Tsubois settled into a somber silence, each of them lost in their own thoughts.

The next order of business was to learn about their surroundings, the most important of which was to find the bathrooms and food. The awful truth was that the Puyallup fairgrounds was never designed to house over 10,000 people, thus it did not have plumbing to support such a mass of humanity. The bathrooms largely amounted to holes in wooden floors placed over open trenches. The stench was overwhelming, and there was no privacy, leading to many folks going in pairs to hold up blankets for each other as they did their business.

Next came finding food, which wasn't hard to do since there were always long lines of people leading to the makeshift mess halls. Unfortunately, it turned out that the food situation was worse than the bathrooms. Where the everyday Japanese diet was made up of rice, fish, fresh vegetables, miso, and soy sauce, none of the food provided was what they were used to. Meat, like Vienna sausages, came out of cans, rice was nowhere to be found, and the cooking was horrendous. They were at the mercy of Army food and cooks whose jobs were measured more in volume than quality.

Louise later recalled one night when trouble was reported in Camp Harmony and a full-scale alert was issued. Believing it to be a riot, the guards pointed their guns at the Japanese internees. As the mob was ordered to disperse, it was determined that it was not a riot at all, but a desperate rush for the toilets due to diarrhea. The camp had served spoiled food that made everyone sick. It was literally a gut-wrenching and pathetic scene. Fortunately, no shots were fired, and nobody was killed by gunfire or the food.

A section of Camp Harmony at the Puyallup Fairgrounds.
Courtesy of the National Archives and Records Administration.

Through it all, the public was told that their incarceration was voluntary. Local newspapers told the townspeople that everything inside Camp Harmony was going smoothly and that the "evacuees were being provided with plenty of healthful nourishing food for all." It was hard to imagine how things could get any worse.

Shiro had never been among so many thousands of people crammed into such a small space in his life, and none of them were allowed to leave. He actually enjoyed meeting new people and lending a hand to those who needed help. As time went on, everyone got more accustomed and sadly accepted their new surroundings and started to come together as a community. As the days went by, Shiro passed the time by hanging out with friends, playing sports, and helping wherever he could. He was also a major flirt and being such a big guy made him easy to spot, especially by admiring young women.

The day Shiro had to have minor surgery on his foot to remove an ingrown toenail was the day Beauty showed up. A makeshift infirmary had been made in one of the barracks and Shiro was forced to stay in bed and off his feet, which drove him crazy. He hated being stuck and had to find a way to bide his time until he could walk again. Being the major flirt that he was, he especially gave his utmost attention to young women who came his way. For Shiro, being stuck in a camp with over 10,000 people had its fringe benefits, including hundreds—if not a thousand or two—young women stuck in there with him. And then along came Louise Tsuboi.

At sixteen-years-old, Louise had also been looking for things to do. Since jobs were hard to come by in Camp Harmony for young women with no formal work experience, she took the first job she could find as a "tray girl" for $8 a month, serving food to those recovering in the infirmary. As she turned the corner, she immediately recognized the handsome young man she was about to serve as the rival high school quarterback. Her heart raced and she almost dropped the tray.

Approaching his bed, Louise realized she had about five seconds to figure out how she should act when she gave Shiro his food. She was attractive and friendly, and he was a bespectacled and handsome guy who had a reputation for being a flirt. She decided to keep her cool and treat him with the same respect and care as she did everyone she served. As she arrived at his bedside, Shiro looked up and suddenly found himself in the presence of a beautiful young woman who carried herself well beyond her age of sixteen.

Straightening himself up in bed, he said hello to Louise with a big smile and thanked her for bringing his food. After some brief conversation, they introduced themselves and became instant friends. Shiro learned that Louise and her family had arrived in Camp Harmony after selling the family store, and the heartbreak her family went through after losing everything. They got to know each other better in the days Shiro was laid up in bed. He even called her "honey," which Louise was sure he did with every girl he was interested in.

Back on his feet, Shiro went back to hanging out with his friends, meeting as many girls as he could, and helping others make Camp

Harmony their new home for now. Because he did not stay with his siblings and had no other family, he was assigned to a bachelor's barrack with a bunch of other single men and spent his time taking care of other families and making new friends. One of his friends, Isamu, mentioned that he wanted to meet Louise. Being the great friend that he was, Shiro said he would be happy to introduce him, even though he really liked Louise himself. He figured that if she felt the same way, she'd find a way to let him know.

Occasionally, dances would be held in Camp Harmony. Shiro, being true to his word, used an upcoming dance to get Louise and Isamu together. Louise accepted Shiro's invitation to the dance. After all, she figured it'd be fun to see if the big, bad quarterback of Garfield High could dance. During their first dance together, Shiro guided Louise toward where Isamu was standing. Louise quickly realized what was going on. When they got close to Isamu and Shiro introduced them, Louise said "Hi," and danced Shiro back to the center of the dance floor. It was clear that as Shiro brought Louise to the dance, Louise was going to make sure he stayed with her and took her home.

As the days went by, folks settled in. New friends were made and communities amongst the barracks started to form and gel. Nobody knew how long they were going to be there, and everyone made do as best they could. While Louise's family liked Shiro very much for his friendliness and leadership, he and Louise were on and off like a light bulb. Being the energetic, gregarious, and adventurous soul that he was, Shiro loved to meet girls and he had many to choose from. This meant major competition for Louise, but it was also a chance for her to meet a lot of boys. So, when they were together, she would treat him with the love and respect he craved. When they were apart, she'd still be nice to him, but she would also drive him crazy with little reminders that he wasn't her boyfriend. Louise could play the flirting game a whole lot better than Shiro, anyway. Their agreement was simple; as long as they weren't together, Shiro could meet other girls and Louise could meet other boys, and she made him hate it.

Mrs. Tsuboi also played the game with Louise. While she always made young people feel welcome, she treated Shiro with the parental love he never had. When he and Louise were apart, Mrs. Tsuboi would make Shiro his favorite sushi to entice him back. Nobody knew how she did it, but she was somehow able to find fresh ingredients and kept Shiro coming back for more. Louise was a fighter, so she wasn't giving up on Shiro anytime soon. When they were together, Shiro and Louise often talked about their friends and families and how what was happening to them was so unfair and dreamed of a better future.

While in Camp Harmony, the vice principal of Broadway High School came to Puyallup to present Louise her diploma. It was sad for her to graduate behind barbed wire without her class, and it was quite the contrast to the pomp and circumstance she dreamed of for her graduation from high school. While receiving her diploma should have been a reason to celebrate, Louise could only cry herself to sleep, hoping for better days ahead. For now, she was a high school graduate in an American military prison.

In July of 1942, two months into their stay in Camp Harmony, a call for volunteers went out to go somewhere in advance of the rest of the internees. Although there were no other details, Shiro was one of the first to volunteer. He figured it could be an opportunity to help set things up for everyone and also provide him with an adventure out of the daily monotony of Camp Harmony. But the one thing that caused him to hesitate was leaving Louise. A budding romance had been born in Camp Harmony, and he wanted to be with her. Despite wanting to stay together, they both decided that perhaps he could do some good on the advanced team, so they agreed that he should go. Two days later, Shiro boarded a train and left Camp Harmony for a destination and fate completely unknown.

4

Home in an American Concentration Camp

As they left Camp Harmony and boarded a train for an unknown destination, Shiro and everyone on board were told by the Army guards to keep the curtains down. Once they got past the Cascade Mountains east of Seattle, they were able to open the curtains. What they saw was nothing but a barren expanse of desert that seemed to go on forever. Where were they going? What was going to happen to them? Although they knew they were to help build camps, nobody had any idea what their future held, or if they even had one. What were the camps for? Were they to live there? Die there? They were told nothing.

After two days of traveling in the stifling hot July sun, the train finally pulled into their final destination outside of Twin Falls, Idaho. When Shiro stepped off the train, he was greeted by an intensely hot desert sun. The heat was almost unbearable and there was no shade. There was nothing but desolation. Sand and sagebrush ruled the land, and they were told that this was to be their new home.

After gathering their belongings, everyone boarded a bus to the camp whose name everyone heard for the first time, Minidoka. When Shiro and the advance team arrived at Minidoka, he was stunned to see a massive area over two miles long and covering over 900 acres, with the construction of wooden barracks nearly complete. The work to build the necessary facilities and housing for 13,000 people was massive, and it was scheduled to be opened in a few short weeks.

Aerial view of the Minidoka internment camp.
Photo courtesy of the National Archives and Records Administration.

Minidoka was divided into forty blocks (or sections) of buildings, with each block accommodating 300 people and consisting of a mess hall, recreation building, latrines, laundry, and twelve barracks. Each of the barracks was 120 feet long and twenty feet wide, with six units of various sizes including two sixteen-by twenty-foot units to house couples or families of three, two twenty-by twenty-foot units to house families of four or five, and two twenty-four-by twenty-foot units to house six to eight people. They had no plumbing, and the barracks were hastily built with fresh pine wood and covered with tar paper, providing no insulation. Each unit had a single lightbulb, a potbelly stove for heat, Army-issued cots, and wool blankets. Although the units were divided, the walls didn't reach the ceilings, reminiscent of the barracks at Camp Harmony, so everything could be heard by all of the residents, as noise and sounds traveled easily across the units.

The twenty-foot-by-one-hundred-twenty-foot barracks were also built for different purposes. Things like offices, schools, churches, libraries, hospitals, stores, bathrooms, mess halls, and community centers were all accommodated by the same type of barrack buildings. In total, there were nearly 600 barracks at Minidoka to accommodate 13,000 people.

The sheer scale of what had to be readied was enormous, and Shiro and the rest of the advance team were instructed that their job was to help finish the barracks in which families, friends, and fellow Japanese Americans would live. He was delighted with the assignment because it kept him busy and gave him an opportunity to help the people by doing a good job of finishing up what would eventually be their homes. It was hard, dirty work in the hot desert sun. Blisters and heatstroke were commonplace as they worked in hundred-plus-degree weather, and the thing they had to be careful of most was dehydration, which could land a man in the infirmary for days. On days when it would rain, the land would turn to mud and the simple act of walking became quite difficult.

Shiro showed himself to be a leader almost immediately, as he encouraged everyone to push through in readying the barracks and facilities. He would often shout "Come on! Let's keep a goin'!" just like his days as quarterback in high school.

Everyone knew they had a deadline to make, so they stayed focused. Occasionally some excitement would break out as a rattlesnake would find its way among the men, or a scorpion was discovered in their shoes. In any case, shovels were quite useful in dispatching both.

Shiro and the men worked seven days a week in the brutally hot sun until the day Minidoka opened. It was an enormous effort, and on August 10, 1942, the Minidoka Internment Camp was opened for its new inhabitants for their incarceration, though it would take another six months to complete the project, during which time the internees had to suffer without proper plumbing and with the now-familiar open trenches for bathroom facilities. The huge military prison camp stood in the Idaho desert, as one would imagine a prison camp in the middle of nowhere. Surrounded by barbed wire and guard towers, it was more reminiscent of a maximum-security prison for hardened criminals and enemy combatants than for families and children.

These camps were not built for people who deserved to be there. Every person there was taken involuntarily by force. As neither life nor civilization seemed to exist in this barren wasteland, it was a harsh and pathetic existence that awaited every man, woman, and child who entered the gates of Minidoka. And to those who said that the camps were built to protect them, one internee would later ask, "If we were there for our protection, why were the guns always pointed at us?"

Back in Camp Harmony, Louise was cautiously optimistic that moving to a new place would be an improvement in their living conditions, but nobody knew what awaited them on the other side. As they boarded the train for the hot, uncomfortable journey to an unknown destination, a great deal of fear and uncertainty permeated through the train cars among the internees. As the soldiers continued to treat them like prisoners, herding them onto the trains like cattle, Louise was relieved to see that the train cars they would be riding in were those used for passengers and not the ones used for livestock.

For two days in the hot train cars, everyone wondered what was to become of them. Some were fearful that they were being taken into the isolation of the desert to be shot. Nobody knew where they were going, what they were going to do, or how long they would be there. They were pathetically hopeless about their future. Louise and her family made the best of their journey and comforted each other when things seemed to be at their worst. She often thought of Shiro and worried about whether he was safe and hoped that he was happy being part of the advance group. It was her anticipation and excitement of seeing him again that sustained her during the grueling train ride across the deserts of Washington and Idaho.

With each train car filled to capacity, they had to make the entire trip sitting upright with nowhere to lie down or stretch out. The train cars felt like ovens in the hot summer sun. Soot from the coal engines filled the air, and the unpleasant mingled scent of human sweat and body odor wafted unavoidably through the sealed train cars. Outside, there was nothing but barren desert and desolation for as far as the eye could see. To add insult to injury, the toilet malfunctioned, and that stench filled the train car, adding to the unpleasant odors that had already permeated the space. Fortunately, other train cars had working toilets.

After two hot days on the sweltering train, everyone was tired, hungry, and covered in black soot from the coal train engine. While Louise did her best to freshen up and brush her hair, there was only so much she could do. Her nervousness and worry about where they were being taken were only exceeded by her excitement about being reunited with Shiro. Louise was sad and depressed to see that the beautiful green trees and cool fresh air of Seattle had been replaced by searing heat and desolation of sand and sagebrush as far as she could see. It was a harsh and unforgiving land that was not meant for human beings, let alone helpless children and the elderly.

They were welcomed by a scorching hot sun, painful to their uncovered skin, and directed to buses that would take them to their final destination, Minidoka. After another hour on the hot bus, Louise and her family were ordered off the bus into what would be their new desert home. As she looked around trying to get her bearings, she heard Shiro call out her name, and was horrified to realize that her face was covered in sweaty soot when Shiro burst out laughing. She was a mess, looking a lot like a clown having a bad makeup day, and he loved her all the more for it.

Shiro had come to pick them up in a truck he was allowed to use since he volunteered to help out in the warehouse. He had no idea which bus the Tsubois would arrive on, so he was there for every arrival hoping to find Louise. As they drove to their assigned barracks, Mr. and Mrs. Tsuboi rode in front with Shiro, and the rest of the family jumped into the back of the truck. Just as they arrived at their barracks, a sandstorm hit as if to welcome the Tsuboi family to their new home. They quickly realized how badly the barracks were built as sand blew in through the gaps between the wall boards and floorboards. It was impossible to keep the sand out, and everyone eventually resigned themselves to the constant presence of sand.

Main entrance to Minidoka. Photo courtesy of Densho.org

When the sandstorm subsided, they emerged from their barracks and Shiro took them around the block that was to be their living community to help them get their bearings. He showed them where everything was, including the bathroom facilities that were yet to be completed, and the mess hall where all meals would be served. The familiar barbed wire fencing and armed soldiers posted in guard towers surrounding Minidoka were the same as Camp Harmony, but what Louise was not prepared for was the desolation. She thought to herself that if anyone were to escape, they would likely die since there was nowhere to go. She felt isolated and detached from the rest of civilization.

Life at Minidoka and the other internment camps got better over time as the internees recovered from their initial shock and settled in and resigned themselves to make the best of their new home. Food was the first priority. What they were being served was terrible. As in Camp Harmony, the camp cooks were ordered to focus on quantity more than quality, and mutton (old sheep) was often served. It had a terrible odor, and many refused to eat it, which made finding better food and provisions a top priority for the inmates. Folks who were cooks and restaurant owners before the war started were employed to take over kitchen and cooking duties to make better and more familiar food. Eventually, everyone came together as a community and started up schools, doctor's offices, hospitals, stores, and other businesses.

Everybody did their part to transform their desert prison into more livable space including gardens, rock pathways, and play areas. Photo courtesy of the National Archives and Records Administration.

With a population of over 13,000, Minidoka became the equivalent of one of the largest towns in Idaho, complete with a fire department, a small police detail, and medical facilities. Jobs became available inside the camp, with common workers paid $8 per month, supervisors paid $12 per month, and doctors and other professionals paid $18 per month. Schools were created where the children attended class every day and recited the Pledge of Allegiance every morning. As unjust as their incarceration was, America was still their country. Gardens were built between the barracks, and they eventually figured out how to irrigate the land of tumbleweeds to grow fruit and vegetable crops for the entire camp. It became everyone's job to make Minidoka as comfortable and livable as possible.

Like Camp Harmony, privacy was terribly lacking for everyone in the camp. There was absolutely no privacy in the bathrooms and showers, so people would wait until late at night to use the facilities or go in pairs so one could hold up a sheet while the other did their business. And finding privacy for intimate moments was especially difficult since the partitions between each unit did not reach the ceiling. The sounds of romance and intimacy carried across the barracks. As well, gaps between the wallboards created concern for curious eyes. It was not uncommon for children to be kicked out of the barracks and left to their own devices when the grown-ups had grown-up things to do.

As time went on, sports leagues and teams started to emerge in camp. Before Executive Order 9066, Seattle had twenty-three Japanese American semi-pro baseball teams, and the enthusiasm for baseball carried into Minidoka. The barren desert was transformed into baseball diamonds, and uniforms were often made of potato sacks. A high school team was formed, along with seven adult baseball teams, from which an All-Star traveling team was selected. Shiro was selected for the All-Star team, which was permitted to play games with teams outside of the camp in the surrounding area, many of which they dominated. As Shiro would later say, "Baseball saved us . . . . through sports you break a lot of barriers . . . . Baseball made our lives easier during a really tough time."

As Shiro's and Louise's relationship continued to blossom, they spent just about all of their free time together, except when Shiro played baseball. Being the fierce and hot-headed competitor that he was, he often used foul language, and sometimes resorted to bending the rules and playing dirty. Since he hated to lose and didn't want Louise to see that side of him, he did not allow Louise to watch him play baseball.

One of Minidoka's baseball teams. Shiro Kashino is in the middle row, second from the right. Photo courtesy of the Kashino family and Densho.org.

Louise eventually decided to bend the rules herself and snuck behind other spectators to watch Shiro play. Sure enough, out came the bad language whenever a bad call was made. In fact, it became something of a pattern; bad calls always made bad language. He was such a competitive guy, and she thought it was kind of cute. Shiro also did some things that were a bit questionable, like blocking third base or tripping up the base runner when the umpire wasn't looking. When the other team would object, he'd just shrug his shoulders and proclaim his innocence. She always laughed and shook her head when he played dirty.

As their love for each other continued to grow, Shiro knew that he had a lot of growing up to do. Like many young men his age, Shiro drank, smoked, and gambled often more than he should, and he knew it. He also realized that if he were to have any chance for a long-term relationship, he would have to learn how to make a good life for Louise and his future family. But most importantly, he had to figure out how to get out of Minidoka, since being incarcerated in an internment camp was no way to live.

While Shiro proved himself to be a great competitor and leader, he also had a reputation of being a bit of a hothead. At Minidoka, Shiro headed a crew in the supply warehouse. One Sunday, when he and his buddies were dressed up and headed for church, the foreman of the warehouse unexpectedly told Shiro that he needed his crew to move meat that had just arrived. Reluctantly, they went to the warehouse in their church clothes to unload the trucks. Since the meat was heavy and awkward to carry, Shiro's team was deliberate and careful not to soil their clothes, causing the foreman to yell at them for working too slowly. Shiro responded by throwing a big chunk of meat at him, knocking the foreman off his feet. The next day, Shiro and his crew were fired.

Shiro knew he was wrong and should have handled the whole situation better. Since the pay was only $12 a month, he didn't really care about the job, but he did care about his crew having been unfairly fired. So, not to be outdone, Shiro told the entire warehouse crew of 120 men about what happened and led a strike in opposition to what they all thought was unfair treatment. Because the warehouse served all of Minidoka, and any kind of shutdown would cause big trouble, Shiro and his team were invited back to work three hours later. It was the only strike that ever happened at Minidoka, and Shiro had led it.

The following month, Shiro got word that farmers in Montana were looking for help to harvest sugar beets. There was a shortage of manpower due to the war, and farmers were desperate for help. Because Montana was outside the military exclusion zone, Japanese Americans who applied for work permits were allowed to leave Minidoka under farmer sponsorship. For Shiro, this offered an opportunity to get out of the camp and make a lot more than $12 a month, so he and a group of his friends were given permission to leave Minidoka to work in the fields of Montana. Of course, while Louise wasn't happy with him leaving, she understood his reasoning and encouraged him to go. Promising to write to each other regularly, Shiro headed to Montana looking forward to his new adventures in farming, something he had never done before.

It was hard, backbreaking work from 5:30 a.m. to sundown. Shiro wrote to Louise two to three times a week, constantly repeating his promise that he would become a better man and build a good life for her. He wrote about farming in Montana and how he had never worked so hard in his life. He loved Louise and cared about her and her family deeply and would jokingly say that "I wouldn't blame you if you find another boy while I'm gone but hope you won't."

But the truth of the matter was that all of Shiro's friends knew that Louise was his girl, so she was basically untouchable. As for Shiro, he wrote of his escapades flirting with beautiful young women in Montana, though he insisted it was always innocent and that he was "reforming" himself to become a much better man for Louise.

So, with her man out chasing young women in Montana, what was Louise to do? For her, one answer was to go dancing. After all, she figured, "What could be more innocent than dancing?"

With Shiro in Montana doing what he wanted to do, Louise decided that it was only fair for her to do what she wanted to do, so she went dancing. Everything was fine until word got to Shiro that Louise was going to dances with other boys. Although he would always say it was okay for her to date other boys, he made it known to them that if they dated Louise, they would have to answer to him. And the problem for Louise was that everyone knew that Shiro was big, strong, and fearless. Worst of all, they all knew that he knew how to fight and viewed pain as a great teacher. Nobody in their right mind would even think of getting on Shiro's bad side, not to mention messing with the love of his life.

It was a conundrum that didn't take Louise very long to figure out. After all, there were 13,000 people in Minidoka spread across 900 acres. The place was huge and spread out literally for miles, and there was no way that everyone in that place knew Shiro. So, what did she do? As she would say later, it was easy; she just met other boys to dance with who didn't know him. In her letters, she was as honest with him as he was with her about meeting beautiful girls. It was her way of making him suffer and keeping him on the straight and narrow, and it drove him crazy.

Louise spent much of her time helping her family and the community and earned some money doing work around the camp. One day, a local farmer requested help harvesting his crops, so Louise and some of her friends decided that it would be a nice way to make some money and experience what Shiro was doing. Little did she know that it would be the hardest and most backbreaking work she had ever done. She thought of her Shiro doing that hard and miserable work but was comforted by knowing that he was doing what he wanted to do and was where he wanted to be. She wanted to quit working after the first day but stayed true to her promise to work for a full week. After she finished her one-week commitment to harvesting crops, she walked away and resolved to develop professional skills so she would never have to do manual work again.

Shiro came back to Minidoka in November of 1942, as fall turned to winter, and the weather turned brutally cold. The winters at Minidoka proved to be unbearable, with temperatures dropping well below freezing on a regular basis. There was no insulation in the barracks, and all that was provided for warmth was a small potbelly stove, which proved to be completely inadequate. But the worst was the torrential rains that would turn the ground into a paste-like mud twelve inches deep, which made it nearly impossible to get to the mess hall and bathroom. They eventually built slightly elevated walkways of basalt gravel, which prevented them from sinking in the mud. But despite the misery of the cold, wet, and snow, everybody made do and took care of each other.

Shiro made his way back to Montana two months later, this time to work on a dairy farm. The cold Montana winter meant that he often couldn't work and had to stay indoors. This was a big lesson for him that Louise also learned at just about the same time as Shiro; that tough, manual work was not something he wanted to do for the rest of his life, especially when he lost his hard-earned money gambling, drinking, and wasting time when the weather kept him inside. If he were to create a secure life for himself and Louise, he would do it less with his brawn and more with his brain as a white-collar worker.

5

For the Sake of the Children

In 1942, as Japanese Americans from the West Coast were being transferred from the assembly centers like Camp Harmony to their respective internment camps, Japanese Americans in Hawaii were experiencing something quite different. In May of 1942, a racially segregated unit of more than 1,400 Japanese Americans who had served in the Hawaii National Guard was established as the 100th Infantry Battalion, and subsequently removed from Hawaii on June 12, 1942, by the War Department due to fear of these soldiers possibly supporting attacks in the Hawaiian Islands by the Japanese Imperial Navy.

For over a year, they went through basic training and intensive vetting in Wisconsin, Louisiana, and Mississippi while the Army decided what to do with them. Finally, in August of 1943, the 100th battalion was deployed and entered combat in Salerno in southern Italy. Because of their outstanding performance during basic training, and the realization that not a single Japanese American had committed espionage or sabotage and could therefore be trusted, the War Department established the 442nd Regimental Combat Team (RCT) in February of 1943, made up mostly of Japanese American volunteers from all over the country, including the Japanese American concentration camps.

In March of 1943, one month after the establishment of the 442nd RCT, Shiro received the notice that the United States Army needed Japanese American volunteers to serve and fight in World War II. Now that President Roosevelt had authorized the formation of the 442nd RCT, many Japanese American men who lived outside the West Coast military exclusion zones and weren't incarcerated in the camps immediately volunteered.

In Hawaii, where the vast majority of Japanese Americans were not subject to any kind of incarceration, nearly 2,700 young men immediately volunteered for the 442nd. Daniel Inouye had plans to become a physician, but like everyone else, his ambitions were changed by the attack on Pearl Harbor and he volunteered to fight for the United States Army along with some of his buddies. But what about the young men in the ten internment camps on the mainland? Was the United States Army seriously expecting them to volunteer?

The call for volunteers from the internment camps was an absurdity. How could the United States government expect anyone in the Japanese American internment camps to volunteer to fight and perhaps die for the same Army that unjustly held them and their families in prison in some of the harshest conditions in America? Who in their right mind would volunteer under such conditions? Shiro would, and he did.

Shiro resolved to volunteer the moment he heard of the formation of the 442nd Regimental Combat Team, and immediately returned to Minidoka, only to find a camp divided. While many in the camp felt strongly that they should resist volunteering for the Army and instead fight the injustice of their incarceration and having their constitutional rights taken away, others were equally passionate about taking every opportunity to prove their loyalty to the United States. It was especially hard for parents who had already lost everything they owned from Executive Order 9066 and now feared their sons being sacrificed. The ensuing debates and arguments within the camp among families and friends caused tremendous tension and heartache within all ten internment camps. Fights that ensued pitted families against families and friends against friends; some relationships of which would never recover.

The No-No Boys

The energy and passion on both sides of the issue tore communities apart in the internment camps. Earlier in the year, the U.S. government had required all men over the age of seventeen to complete a questionnaire titled "Statement of U.S. Citizenship of Japanese American Ancestry," which included two key questions:

> Question 27: Are you willing to serve in the armed forces of the United States on combat duty, wherever ordered?

> Question 28: Will you swear unqualified allegiance to the United States of America and faithfully defend the United States from any or all attacks by foreign or domestic forces, and forswear any form of allegiance or obedience to the Japanese emperor, or any other foreign government, power, or organization?

The answers to questions 27 and 28 were used to judge a person's loyalty to the United States of America. Photo courtesy of the National Archives and Records Administration.

There were men who answered "no" to both questions (i.e., No-No) for a variety of reasons. For question 27, many could not imagine going to war for the same government that imprisoned them and their families in a concentration camp for no other reason than their ancestry. For question 28, many answered "no" because forswearing allegiance could have implied that they had allegiance to Japan.

Those who answered no to both questions were later referred to as the "No-No Boys" and were considered dangerous and disloyal by the United States government. For having done nothing more than answering a questionnaire and committing no crime whatsoever, the No-No Boys were handcuffed and transferred to a maximum-security prison in California, the Tule Lake Segregation Center. While it was hard to imagine, life for these men in Tule Lake became worse than their lives in Minidoka.

Shiro knew exactly what he was going to do. He had answered "yes" to both questions and figured that serving in the United States Army would not only get him out of Minidoka, but would also be the best way to prove his grit and loyalty to America. While many in the camp were saying that he and the other volunteers were going out of sheer bravado, it wasn't that simple. All of them thought deeply about volunteering and about the future, and Shiro felt that he had no choice. He spoke with Louise about how important it was that he prove his loyalty as an example for all Japanese Americans. He felt that failure to do so would serve as proof of the government's suspicions that they were not loyal to the United States. He knew he had to volunteer. His home was an internment camp in Idaho, and he thought it would be terrible for him and his future family to have to live like that forever. He and other Japanese Americans had to prove themselves, so they could get back to a normal life again. This was his country, and he was an American.

Shiro was also very sympathetic to the parents of the sons who wanted to volunteer after having lost everything they had worked decades for when they were forcibly removed from their homes. Now their sons were volunteering to fight and die for the Army that had destroyed their lives. With no parents to worry about him, Shiro felt he had less to lose and was more expendable than the other young men whose parents would be so heartbroken if their sons died. Every one of the volunteers knew they could die, and that in the event of their death during battle, their families would be presented with an American flag and a Gold Star by a contingent of U.S. Army officers within the barbed wire fences of Minidoka and the other internment camps. It was difficult to comprehend.

Louise bravely accepted Shiro's decision as they sat together in silence reflecting on what the future would hold for them. As sad as she was, Louise refused to cry because she didn't want to make it any harder for Shiro than it already was. He was to leave her behind to fight—and maybe die—for the very government that had so wrongly put him and Louise in the internment camp they were sitting in at that very moment. He submitted his application for the Army and waited to be called up.

It was also in March of 1943 that the United States government decided to allow internees who were cleared by the FBI and could prove that they had a reason to leave the camps to relocate to the Midwest or East Coast. In addition to the 100th Battalion of Japanese Americans proving their worth in the U.S. military, not a single person of Japanese ancestry had been convicted of spying or doing harm to the United States. So although being released to return to the West Coast was not an option due to Executive Order 9066, and the military exclusion zones still being in place, moving to other parts of the country was allowed.

Because Louise had already finished high school, the Tsubois were anxious for her to continue her education and encouraged her to take advantage of this program. The following month, Louise received news that she had been approved for sponsorship to live with a Quaker family and attend business school in Chicago. Her mother, who had the highest of expectations for all her children, made the arrangements, and Louise was permitted to leave Minidoka and start a new life in Chicago since it was outside the West Coast military exclusion zone.

Shiro was heartbroken that Louise was leaving him to start a new life, and with both of them knowing that Shiro could be sent off to war at any time, they also realized that they may never see each other again. But they also knew that any opportunity for Louise to leave Minidoka and start a normal life was an opportunity not to forego. So, at seventeen-years-old and with a suitcase filled with all of her worldly possessions in hand, Louise promised to write often and said goodbye to Shiro and her family in Minidoka and started her journey on her own as she boarded a train to Chicago.

The train to Chicago was a much different experience than the train to Minidoka. It was clean, comfortable, and absent of Army guards. Instead of having a feeling of fear and dread for what lay ahead, Louise was now excited for her new adventure in Chicago. She was now free to do as she wished, as long as she didn't return to the West Coast, which was still under the jurisdiction of the United States Army. But as happy as she was to be released from Minidoka, having left Shiro and her family behind was one of the hardest things she had ever done. Now she was on her own to make a new life for herself in a city she knew nothing about.

Louise found Chicago to be a bustling city much bigger and busier than Seattle. While she expected the people in Chicago to be as prejudiced toward her as they were in Seattle, she was pleasantly surprised by how nice and helpful folks were as she navigated her way to the Quaker family's home. The host family welcomed Louise and were truly kind and made every effort to help and take care of her. They understood and appreciated the hardships that she had experienced as a Japanese American on the West Coast, and that Chicago was a whole new world for her. They took a liking to her right away, as she did her best to fit in. Starting her new life and quickly becoming familiar with her new surroundings, Louise only stayed with them until she found other, more permanent accommodations, but she was always grateful for their help and hospitality.

Louise and Shiro wrote to each other regularly, with Shiro often talking about getting married in the future, but also teasing Louise about the girls he was seeing back in camp, and Louise always kept Shiro straight by telling him he wasn't good enough for her and that she was meeting boys in Chicago, even though she wasn't. In the meantime, Shiro's application to volunteer for the Army was being held back for some reason. Many folks suspected that it was because of the warehouse strike he led that branded him a troublemaker. Finally, in September 1943, Shiro's application was accepted, and the first order of business was for him to pass the physical examination. This concerned him greatly, since his eyesight was so bad and he couldn't function without his glasses. As one of his friends put it, without his glasses he was as blind as a bat. Shiro knew that if he took an honest eye exam, he would surely fail and would never be allowed into the Army.

He heard stories of guys who had failed the eye exam. One volunteer was given the answers by guys who had taken the exam and memorized the chart. Confident that he was sure to pass, the volunteer walked in, looked at the wall, and accurately called out the letters. Unfortunately, the eye chart was on a different wall. Another memorized the answers only to be congratulated for reciting the letters of the eye chart that was replaced the day before. Shiro knew he needed help to pass the eye exam, so when the time came, he went with his friend, Masao Watanabe, who pointed him toward the proper wall so that he would be facing the eye chart and then proceeded to whisper the letters to him. They were sure that they would be busted, but the recruiter said that anyone that desperate to join the Army had his approval and congratulated Shiro on passing the eye exam. After that, the rest was smooth sailing. He was tall, big, healthy, strong, and determined; exactly what the U.S. Army wanted in a soldier.

As lonely as she was in Chicago, Louise stayed strong. Shiro was going to war because that was the kind of man he was; always fighting for what he believed was right. Their relationship had grown to where they loved each other deeply, but they both knew that going to war for America was the right thing for Shiro to do. He and the other 305 men from Minidoka settled their affairs and prepared themselves for their dangerous journey ahead. It was by far the largest number of volunteers out of any of the ten internment camps.

It was a long series of trains and buses that brought Shiro to a place 120 miles north of New Orleans and just outside the town of Hattiesburg, Mississippi. It was a sprawling U.S. Army base where the 442nd Regimental Combat Team was assembled for basic training, with sand and pine trees as far as the eye could see and stiflingly hot and humid weather in the summers. The place was massive. The buildings and barracks were old and dilapidated, and the latrine was 100 yards away from the barracks, with open toilets and no privacy. It was described by some of the men as miserable, and it was to be the home for the men of the 442nd for their basic training. In many respects, Shiro found it worse than Minidoka. This was Camp Shelby.

It was 1943, and most of the Japanese American volunteers had experienced discrimination against them, but they never experienced the kind of racism and segregation that was common throughout the south where Jim Crow laws enforced segregation and mandated separate facilities and accommodations for whites and African Americans, including public restrooms, hospitals, and schools. In town, it wasn't uncommon for white store owners to refuse service to Black people. Bathrooms were marked as Whites Only or Blacks Only—and never did the two intermix. This initially created a problem for the Japanese American men of the 442nd, because they didn't know which bathroom to use. They would all eventually learn that they were to consider themselves as whites, though some of the men would frequent the Black bathrooms just to annoy the white people. For many of the men of the 442nd, it just didn't make sense.

Buses were also segregated, with the whites sitting in front and Blacks sitting in the back. When a Black soldier was denied entry on a bus because the Black section was completely full, some men of the 442nd who were on the bus asked the driver to let him aboard. They pleaded with the driver to let the soldier sit with them. After all, he was in uniform and serving in the same Army. The conversation evolved into an argument, and when the driver continued to refuse, they beat him up. Such were the kinds of cultural differences the Japanese American men of the 442nd would have to adjust to.

Shiro would later recall that in the early days of the 442nd, fights often broke out in Hattiesburg as the Japanese Americans learned about their new surroundings. At first, many residents of Hattiesburg did not want the Japanese Americans in or around their community, which resulted in hard feelings. It was so bad that the town was almost made off-limits to the men of the 442nd, but as time went on, cooler heads and understanding prevailed. Although there continued to be pockets of scuffling and situations where store and homeowners would refuse service to the Japanese Americans, the men of the 442nd proved themselves to be good and generous guests and were treated well in Hattiesburg.

Shiro entered Camp Shelby with his buddy Tadao Hayashi, who volunteered out of the concentration camp in Poston, Arizona, and both were assigned to "I Company" of the 3rd Battalion. The commander of I Company was 2nd Lieutenant Joseph Byrne, who Shiro would learn to respect immensely. Most of the officers were white, many of whom were not happy with their assignments in a segregated "Jap" unit, but Joseph Byrne was an exception. And for many of the volunteers of the 442nd, the white commanders of Camp Shelby reminded them of the internment camp guards and plantation owners back in Hawaii, where many of the Hawaiian men had worked and lived.

Fights often broke out between white soldiers and the men of the 442nd. George Morihiro, who would become part of Shiro's squad, recalled a situation when a bunch of white soldiers in Camp Shelby yelled "dirty Japs!" and ran for their lives as the Japanese Americans charged at them with their rifles and bayonets. Discrimination against the Japanese Americans did not stop, even when they wore American uniforms.

One of the big problems that the Army was unprepared for was the need for small uniforms and boots, since the average height of the Japanese American men was a mere five feet four inches. They had to make do with standard sized uniforms and boots that were far too large for them. As well, the Hawaiians required extra wide boots. Because they wore slippers their entire lives, their feet grew without the constraints of shoes and the Army did not have boots in wide enough sizes to suit them properly. The oversized clothes and poorly fitting boots would cause problems in battle that no other soldiers would have to suffer.

Lieutenant Byrne's favorite soldier to pick on was Takeshi "Shorty" Kazumura, who lived up to his name. Standing at four feet nine inches, his uniform was way too big on him. Even as he tucked in his pants and rolled up his sleeves, he looked more like a grade school child wearing his dad's clothes than a soldier. The Army issued him size eight boots, which were far too big and narrow for him. When Byrne asked him how he got into the Army, Shorty told him that an error in the paperwork showed his height at five feet eight inches, so he went ahead and volunteered after witnessing two of his good friends get blown up at Pearl Harbor.

Over time, the Japanese American men of the 442nd settled into their life in Camp Shelby, including learning to live with the racism levied toward them. But despite the racial conflicts, the greatest challenge faced by the 442nd was not rooted in the racism of others against them, but in the differences between the Japanese American men from Hawaii and the Japanese American men from the mainland; they despised each other.

Shiro and Tadao were big guys who got along well with everyone, including the guys from Hawaii. And since they towered over most of the Hawaiians, nobody messed with them. Shiro always smiled and laughed and never got mad. Everyone liked Shiro and Tadao, mainlanders and Hawaiians alike, but they were more the exception than the rule.

Most of the men from Hawaii came with their buddies and carried big bankrolls from their families who were not incarcerated in internment camps and were able to continue their lives and livelihoods in Hawaii in relative normalcy. They played cards, joked around, and sang songs with their ukuleles. Many of the mainlanders, on the other hand, came from the concentration camps where their families had lost everything they owned, and most did not have their buddies with them. They were alone and insecure, and they certainly didn't have the money the Hawaiians had. So the Hawaiians were viewed as happy-go-lucky gangs of buddies, while the mainlanders were viewed as uptight and stuck-up loners.

Occasionally a group of Hawaiians would be playing cards and buying drinks for their friends while a mainlander would be drinking alone in a corner and would not offer to buy drinks for the Hawaiians. Unbeknownst to the Hawaiians, whose families often sent them spending money, many of the mainland men sent much of their $15 monthly pay to their families in the internment camps, so the last thing they could afford was to buy drinks for the other men.

Another big difference was that the Hawaiians spoke Pidgin English, which blended many different languages, and were dark-skinned from working in the sugar cane and pineapple fields, while the mainlanders were of fair complexions and spoke the Queen's English much like the well-spoken plantation bosses back in Hawaii. There were many occasions when a Hawaiian would talk to a mainlander, who simply didn't understand what they were saying. "Go stay, go" meant "You should leave." "Wassamatta you?" meant "What's wrong with you?" and "Ey, you one fucking kotonk, eh?" meant "Hey, you're a mainlander, right?"

Unfortunately, the Hawaiians incorrectly concluded that the mainlanders didn't respect them because of their Pidgin English, so, as Daniel Inouye would later explain, "If any of those mainland Japanese guys even looked at us funny, KA-POW! One of us would clock him."

On several occasions, mainlanders found out the hard way that misinterpreting or misunderstanding the Hawaiians often meant getting beaten up. It became so bad that the Hawaiians would sometimes attack mainlanders after lights-out while they slept. In one instance, one of the mainlanders was asked "Like beef?" by one of the Hawaiians. Since he liked beef, he mistakenly answered "Yes." Unfortunately, "Like beef?" was Pidgin for "You wanna fight?" That night after lights-out, some of the Hawaiian men snuck into the mainlander's barrack and pummeled him as he slept in his bunk.

Because the groups didn't understand each other, fights between the Hawaiians and Japanese American mainlanders happened on a regular basis. Gangs of Hawaiians would beat up guys they felt were disrespecting them. So bad was the rivalry that the mainlanders called the Hawaiians "Buddhaheads" or "Butaheads" (buta is Japanese for pig), and the Hawaiians called the mainlanders "Kotonks," because when you smacked their heads or their heads hit the ground, it made a hollow sound like "Kotonk!"

The Hawaiians gave everyone a nickname. Shiro got a nickname that would stay with him for the rest of his life: "KASH." From that day on and forevermore in the 442nd, Shiro Kashino would be known as Kash, and Tadao Hayashi would be known as "Beanie" because he had long legs like whites, who they called "Beans" at the camp. Sometimes their chosen nicknames had obvious reasons, and other

Shiro "Kash" Kashino was respected and loved by his men, and always did what he could to keep his men safe, including taking on the most dangerous assignments himself. Photo courtesy of the Kashino family.

times they made no logical sense at all.

The animosity between the Hawaiians and mainlanders got so bad that the regimental commanders thought they would have to disband the entire 442nd Regimental Combat Team all together. They tried everything; social hours, discussion groups, and anything they could think of to bring the men together. Nothing worked. Then, one of the commanders came up with the idea of having the Hawaiians invited to a party in Arkansas. This is how the late Senator Daniel Inouye described the experience:

There was one Hawaiian selected from each of the barracks, and I was lucky to be chosen to go to this party at a camp. So, we all loaded up in the trucks and on our way there we sang songs, played our ukuleles, and celebrated our good fortune in going to a dance to meet young women. Then, on our journey we came around a bend in the road and saw what looked like an Army camp. None of us knew of an Army camp in the area, and then we saw barbed wire and armed guards all around the camp. It was a prison.

What surprised us was that instead of going straight past that facility, we turned right and went directly towards the main entrance. Everyone went dead silent; we all thought we were going to be thrown in prison for some reason. When the truck stopped at the main entrance, we all got out and I looked around the truck and peered inside the main gate. I saw people peering back, and they looked just like me.

None of us from Hawaii had any idea of the Japanese American internment camps. We were invited in and welcomed by the Japanese American families who were imprisoned there by the government we were about to go to war for. All of us expected to have a jolly good time dancing and singing with the young girls, and the families who hosted us wanted us to have a wonderful time. They even offered all their rations and their bunks for us to sleep in. We had no idea this was happening on the mainland and felt terrible. So, we all put on our best faces to act like we were having a good time, but instead of accepting their invitation to sleep in their barracks, we all slept in the trucks instead.

The next day we traveled back to Camp Shelby. During that entire trip not a word was spoken, not a song was sung. We were all left with our own private thoughts about what we had just learned and experienced. And I think all of us were wondering the same thing; would we have volunteered if we were in one of those camps? And I can honestly say that to this day, I don't know. I might very well have said "Nuts to you."

When we arrived back at Camp Shelby, all of us went back to our barracks and explained what happened and what we learned about the Japanese American internment camps, and that the Kotonks had their families in these camps. From that point on there were no more fights, and it was that night the Kotonks became our brothers and the 442nd was born.

The training in Camp Shelby was tough. The twenty-five-mile hikes were particularly tough, and everyone was expected to keep up the grueling pace set by Lieutenant Byrne. It was especially tough for Shorty, since every step the other men took required two from him, which meant he was running most of the time. When it looked as if

Shorty couldn't keep up, Kash and the others would pick him up by his belt and carry him along while another big guy carried his rifle. This way, Shorty was able to finish with the unit and avoid collective punishment, the bane of all Army units.

As the men trained in Camp Shelby, they were given furloughs to visit their families or do whatever they wished. Some of the men went sightseeing around the country, while others visited their families who were still incarcerated in the internment camps. Kash spent his first furlough in Chicago visiting Louise, and they had a great time together. Kash shared his experiences at Camp Shelby with Louise, the most important of which was his new name, Kash. He actually liked it and was told that the Hawaiians gave him the name out of their respect for him. Louise was fascinated to learn about the cultural differences between the Buddhaheads and Kotonks, and was happy to learn that Kash was getting along so well with everyone. She loved going to secretarial school and learning new skills to work in an office. She never forgot the one week she picked crops for the local farmers, and knew she never wanted to do that again, so she worked hard learning office skills that would serve her for the rest of her life.

Kash with Louise during his furlough to Chicago. Photo courtesy of the Kashino family.

When the time came for Kash to leave Chicago and finish up his training in Camp Shelby, Louise knew that it would be the last time for them to be together before he shipped off to war. She hoped his men would take care of him, as she knew he would take care of them. And as they parted, she again promised to keep him apprised of her new life in Chicago, and Kash promised to write her as much as he could.

As the winter turned into spring, the men knew that they would soon be ready for war. They were trained in everything they needed to know about warfare and survival, including hard marches, machine gun training, bayonet fighting, survival training, conditioning, and combat tactics.

The Japanese American men of the 442nd RTC; these men from Hawaii, the mainland, and the Japanese American internment camps; these men who were hated by their white counterparts and countrymen; these Hawaiian and mainland men who nearly destroyed each other before ever facing the enemy; these men who somehow transformed the 442nd RCT into a fierce and widely feared fighting unit, adopted the Hawaiian crapshooter's slogan of "Go for Broke" as its motto. In May of 1944, they were ready to go and entered the war as one of the fiercest fighting units of World War II.

When they received the order to ship out, the men of the 442nd were battle-ready and trained for war. Through it all, every man

1st Squad. First Row: Champ Kawasai, Tommy Umeda, Mickey Akiyama, Blackie Kinoshita, Larry Kazumura, Harry Kuwahara, Masa Manabe. Second Row: Sadaichi Kubota, David Matsuura, Kash, Beanie Hayashi, Mike Takemoto, Masa Kobashigawa, Fred Matsumura. Photo courtesy of I-Company 442nd Veterans Club.

showed a spirit and resolve to not fail. "Go for Broke" meant a lot of different things to the men. But to all of the men, it meant to give it your all and to never hold back on the battlefield. They were all there to fight for America and prove their patriotism, not only for themselves, but for the sake of the children and future generations of Japanese Americans.

The journey from Camp Shelby to their first deployment in Italy was long and dangerous. For the Hawaiian men, crossing the Pacific on a transport ship to the mainland U.S. was bad enough, but now they were crossing the treacherous Atlantic Ocean, which was even rougher than the Pacific and had the added danger of being attacked by enemy ships or submarines. During their ten day journey across the Atlantic, the men passed the time readying themselves, playing cards, and telling stories about home. Kash would let the guys read Louise's letters occasionally; at least the ones that weren't too personal. They admired him for having a girl back home who cared about him so much, and reading her letters made them want to meet her in person.

The Atlantic crossing gave Kash time to think about Louise. No letters were being sent or received while they were on the ship, so he often wondered how she was doing. He knew that she had put on a brave face, telling him that she would be fine in Chicago, but he also knew the reality that she was only eighteen years old in a strange new city, and tried not to worry about her too much. The long voyage also gave him time to reflect on how much he loved her, and he couldn't help but think of the many times he was a real jerk to her; especially when he had chased other young women when he and Louise weren't officially together.

He thought about Louise's family and how loving and inviting they had been to him, and how her mom and dad stepped in to be the parents he didn't have growing up. They had lost everything they had worked their entire life for and had no idea what their future held, as they were still imprisoned in Minidoka. He knew Louise was the girl for him and vowed to become a better man so he could deserve to ask for her hand in marriage when he returned from the war, and to do his best to take care of her parents as well. In the meantime, he realized that it all depended on him surviving the dangerous and bloody conflict that was World War II, and Louise was his reason for coming home in one piece.

Kash had been promoted to Staff Sergeant in I Company. He had proven himself to be a gutsy and courageous leader, but the thing that stood out about Kash was how much he cared about the men. He was always out front encouraging everyone shouting, "Let's keep a-goin'!" and helping anyone who needed help, no matter what the situation. Kash had gained a reputation for being more intense than just about anyone else and always led by example by always going first. He felt a tremendous responsibility to get his men back home alive to their moms and dads, and never expected his men to do anything that he wasn't willing to do himself; and he usually did do the most dangerous and difficult things himself, mostly because he didn't want them to be killed.

The men under Kash's command were all crystal clear in his expectations of them. First, *never retreat*. His view was that if anyone was going to retreat, it was going to be the enemy. Second, *never lose a battle*. In sports and in life, Kash learned that there's always a way to beat your opponent, which was always about outthinking and psyching them out, and the hardest part was having to play by the rules. Now that the only main rule outside the Geneva Convention was "Kill or be killed," Kash knew they'd always figure out how to win. And third, *never leave a wounded or dead man behind*. George Morihiro would later report that, "while Kash was a little crazy, I was never scared of the war under him."

Kash (front row center) with some of his men including Beanie Hayashi on his left. Photo courtesy of the Kashino family.

The 442nd was assigned to General Mark Clark's 5th Army. Their first battle experience happened shortly after they landed in Italy. As they marched and advanced toward Salerno, the men saw the carnage of war as they passed dead civilians, Germans, and body parts scattered across the countryside. Many had never seen or experienced the stench of death before and suddenly realized their own precarious balancing act between life and death; that it could all end for them in the blink of an eye.

Advancing toward Salerno, the locals had informed the Americans that the Germans had left the area. Kash led the first squad of I Company along an upper trail, while other units of the 442nd took other paths toward the city. As he proceeded up to a high wall, he suddenly and unexpectedly came face to face with a German soldier. They simultaneously exchanged fire and the German fell dead to

Kash's Tommy gun, though a bullet grazed Kash's head, momentarily stunning him. When he recovered his senses, he immediately made his way back to the rear where the aid station was located.

This was Kash's first time in combat. Although he wasn't killed, his injury was enough to get him sent to a field hospital. While some of his men didn't expect him to come back, the idea of being sent home because of an injury never entered Kash's mind. All he could think of was getting back to his men in the 442nd. He wrote to Louise several times and never let on that he was ever in danger. He certainly didn't tell her that he was almost killed and got shot in the head in his first firefight and kept his letters light and drama-free so Louise wouldn't worry. But Louise would later learn that Kash writing to her on Red Cross stationery meant he was injured enough to land in the hospital.

As Kash was recovering from his injury, an officer from the 442nd told him that they were being moved to France and that he could join them later. Kash said "Hell no!" and immediately got his clothes and took off from the hospital without permission so he could stay with the 442nd. This "reverse AWOL"—Absent Without Leave—was to become something of a trademark for Kash and the men of the 442nd; to get injured, get patched up, and take off to rejoin his men before anyone could stop him. He had no intention of going home and didn't want to risk being assigned anywhere else. So, he caught up with the 442nd and headed to France to join his men in battle.

6

Save the Texans

In the summer of 1944, the combat team was on R&R (rest and relaxation) on the outskirts of Vada, Italy, after a tough battle experience from Civitavecchia to Rosignano. It was at this time that Barney Hajiro, a private from Hawaii, was reassigned to I Company after having been court-martialed for beating up an Italian. According to Hajiro, he was returning to his company when he saw an Italian beating one of the 442nd soldiers. Hajiro immediately interceded and bloodied the Italian. Just then, the military police appeared and apprehended Hajiro. He explained to the MPs that he got involved only to help a fellow soldier from getting beaten up, but when asked to produce the soldier, the soldier was nowhere to be found. Hajiro was summarily court-martialed and booted out of M Company with the reputation of being a SNAFU ("Situation Normal, All Fucked Up").

Kash immediately accepted and welcomed Barney into his squad. Perhaps it was because of his affinity toward stray dogs and people in need, or his own experience of wishing he could have been part of a real family. Whatever the case, Kash welcomed Barney, who told him, "Sarge, I'm not a bad guy, I go fight only 'cuz one of us boys was getting beat. I'm not a bad guy . . . I going show you someday… I'm not a bad guy."

By October of 1944, the battles in France were becoming far more intense and desperate for the Germans as each Allied victory in France took them yet another step closer to the German homeland. To aid in the heavy fighting in France, the 442nd was reassigned to the 36th Texas Division under the command of General John Dahlquist to break through enemy lines that the Germans were holding strong. Kash and his men were under the command of Lt. Colonel A. Pursell.

The 442nd arrived outside the small French town of Bruyeres, which was strategically located with three main roads running through it. The Germans occupied Bruyeres, and the 36th Texas Division was at a stalemate, fighting the Germans just outside of town. The arrival of the 442nd fortified the forces of the 36th Division to advance through the hills and forests surrounding the town as I and L Companies entered Bruyeres to force the Germans out. It was the worst battle Kash had experienced, as the Germans fought desperately to hold the town. Fighting through the forest and hills surrounding the town, they fought from tree to tree, with the Germans holding the higher ground in dug-in positions that they had prepared weeks ahead of time.

Taking the battle into the town involved moving from building to building to flush the Germans out. Many of the townspeople remained in the basements of their destroyed homes and helped the Americans by letting them know where the Germans were. The fighting was ferocious as the Germans fought to prevent yet another Allied victory toward their homeland, but the Japanese Americans fought successfully and liberated the small town.

As the 442nd was fighting in and around Bruyeres, another effort to advance was happening in the Vosges Forest outside of Bruyeres, where 275 U.S. soldiers known as the famed "Texas Battalion," also under General Dahlquist, were advancing into German lines. They were ordered by Dahlquist to advance aggressively in his quest toward

Germany. But the men of the Texas Battalion had moved too fast and advanced too far as they fell into a trap. The Germans let the Texas Battalion move forward until they got so far ahead that the Germans simply moved in from behind and cut them off from the rest of the division. Suddenly, 700 Germans surrounded them. The Texas Battalion was trapped, and soon became known as the "Lost Battalion." Unless they were saved, their extermination was all but certain.

October 27–30, 1944

For the Japanese Americans' overwhelming victory in the brutal battle to liberate and clear the town of Bruyeres and the surrounding area of Germans, the men of the 442nd were granted some well-deserved time to rest. The epic battle of Bruyeres pushed the men to their physical and mental limits, and now they were given time to recover and recharge for the next campaign. Many of them suffered from malnourishment, as well as ill-fitting boots and equipment. Others suffered from trench foot, a condition that occurs when the feet are wet for prolonged periods of time, causing swelling and blistering followed by skin and tissue dying and falling off, making it excruciatingly painful to walk.

Exhausted and hurting from the battles that raged in Bruyeres up until the previous day, the men of the 442nd were desperate for rest and reinforcements. Kash's head was still ringing from the brick that had hit his head when an artillery shell hit a building, so being given some time to rest was a welcome relief. But before some of the men could even take a shower, the order came for them to move out for immediate action in the Vosges Forest just outside of Bruyeres. They were to pick up where their counterparts in the 2nd and 3rd battalions left off in their efforts to save the Lost Battalion.

While many of the men of the 442nd felt like expendable "cannon fodder," Kash considered it more as an opportunity for the Japanese American men of the 442nd to make a name for themselves and prove their courage and loyalty to the United States of America. He knew that the 442nd RCT, this segregated Army unit of Japanese Americans, who were despised and distrusted by their own country, was the only combat team who would and could succeed. They never backed down from the enemy and hadn't lost a single battle, and the top commanders knew it. Now the 442nd was being ordered to rescue the Lost Battalion as the Army's last resort. Rest or no rest, the order to move out was their new reality, and every man who was able to walk and carry a gun was to be used for the impending battle and rescue. Even cooks and band members of the 442nd suddenly became part of the infantry fighting force.

The Vosges Forest was a dense quagmire of eighty-foot pine trees and brush so thick that it made some areas impossible to navigate. At night, the seemingly unending forest of pine trees loomed overhead, blocking any light filtered by heavy cloud cover, and the dense underbrush made it difficult to maneuver and nearly impossible to see the enemy. Unlike Italy, where they generally knew where the enemy was located, the Vosges Forest and the hilly terrain of dense brush made it so difficult that the enemy could be anywhere; in front, back, side, or even underneath them. Machine gun nests and foxholes were so thoroughly camouflaged that the men of the 442nd were often unaware of them until they were on top of them.

The only thing that exceeded the difficulty of the terrain was the unforgiving weather. It was late October, and the freezing temperatures along with the heavy rain, fog, and mud made it impossible to stay dry. Socks would never dry out in their wet boots, which led to more trench foot. They were constantly cold and shivering and their fingers would go numb. To many of the men, especially those from Hawaii, it must have felt like the coldest

October in history. But through all the misery, death, and hardship that would be thrown at them, their fighting spirit would never diminish.

As they prepared for battle, Kash once again reminded the men in his squad that there would be no retreat, that they would not lose a battle, and that no man would be left behind. As always, he would lead his men into battle and do his best to keep his men alive, even when it meant putting himself at greater risk. He was determined to have all the men under his command go home to their families.

Battle of the Lost Battalion: Day One, October 27, 1944

At 4 a.m. on October 27, 1944, Chaplain Masao Yamada gathered the leaders together for a prayer after the final briefing. The 442nd moved into the pre-dawn blackness of the forest, wading through rain and slush into what seemed like a pitch-black freezing swamp.

There was no moonlight as thick storm clouds blocked any chances of light from above to filter through. It was so dark that the men had to hold onto the backpack of the man ahead because they couldn't even see the man right in front of them. The freezing mud was ankle deep as it soaked into the men's leather boots. The freezing cold made conditions miserable, numbing the hands and feet of every man.

Quietly advancing, I Company slowly and ever so cautiously moved up a ravine. Without warning, a German was heard yelling "Achtung!" and all hell broke loose. The Germans opened fire with their machine guns, and everybody hit the ground. The Germans had taken full advantage of their knowledge of the terrain and launched a surprise attack on the 442nd. The enemy was everywhere, and I Company was heavily hit as bullets seemed to be flying from all directions.

It was hard to see anything since the terrain was thick with dense ground cover, and the enemy was well dug in and camouflaged.

The forest erupted in explosions as the Germans commenced artillery fire with pinpoint accuracy. The artillery shells exploded eighty feet above them at treetop levels, spitting out red-hot, jagged steel and splintered wood from the trees, combining into deadly shrapnel that rained down on the men of the 442nd. These dreaded "tree bursts" created a wider and much more destructive kill zone than bombs exploding on the ground. What was before a silent forest had turned into a living hell.

After getting his bearings as the initial battle raged on, Kash moved forward to lead the charge. His heart pounding, he desperately looked to identify enemy positions. He spotted the gun flashes of an enemy machine gun nest that had his men pinned down. Bombs exploded all around the men and tree bursts exploded above them. With no regard for his own safety, Kash stayed crouched low to the ground and moved slowly toward the machine gun nest like a cat inching toward its prey, using the dense bush to cover his advance. He had to be careful of landmines and booby traps as he suddenly launched his assault, wiping out a machine gun nest with two Germans. He immediately took cover to avoid being hit by a German sniper and checked on each of his men to make sure they were all okay and called for a medic for those who were injured.

The men of the 442nd slowly but surely pushed forward. It was a massive battle. Where the Germans had months to dig their foxholes, the men of the 442nd had mere seconds to protect themselves from snipers and machine gun fire. But the ground underneath them at that point was so cold and hard that they were not able to dig in, and sniper fire forced them to stay low. The sound of exploding trees all around them was beyond deafening as the Germans barraged the men of the 442nd with artillery fire, raining burning wood and shrapnel on them. They were sitting ducks.

The men were desperate to find cover. As Kash quickly moved from man to man, a tree burst exploded above him and a large tree limb fell to the ground, instantly killing the man next to him. It was only a matter of inches that made the difference between life and death, but he had no time to think about it. The Germans were impossible to see and firing on the Japanese American soldiers with pinpoint accuracy. Kash knew that the only way to get the enemy to expose their positions with gunfire flashes was to expose himself first. He quickly dashed from man to man in ten-foot spurts, drawing enemy fire and pushing his men forward yelling, "Let's keep a goin'!"

Kash sprinted fifty yards up a hill, exposing himself to the enemy in order to help a platoon pinned down in front of him. When he saw some of the men pull back on the verge of withdrawing, Kash yelled at them to hold ground and fight back. Then, shouting to his comrades to follow, he covered their movement and directed their fire against another enemy machine gun, enabling the men to escape the kill zone. Kash was characteristically the last to leave, making sure everyone else was safe. His command held the company together and averted a major disaster. He would later be regarded as one of the most gallant soldiers of the 442nd.

During the battle, Kash took cover with Kazuo "Gus" Murakami. He told Gus that there was something on his back and asked him to take a look. As Kash took off his backpack, careful to keep his head down, it didn't take long for Gus to see that Kash was losing blood through a big shrapnel hole in Kash's back that clearly required medical attention. Gus told Kash that he had a big hole in his back and that he should get it patched up. Despite his reluctance and protests in having to leave his men on the battlefield, Kash finally agreed with Gus and disengaged from the battle and quickly made his way back to the aid station.

The Germans counterattacked in force. Death and dying was happening all around. As one of the 442nd soldiers followed in the rear, he stopped in his tracks as he came across a German arm sticking out of the ground, its body half buried. Bodies were everywhere. The German artillery barrages continued, and many men of the 442nd were wounded and killed from tree bursts. Sixty years later, Mitsuo Yakuma would still dream about body parts in tree branches. Bodies were part of the trees, and trees were part of bodies. The carnage was everywhere.

By the end of that first intense day of battle, the 442nd had taken over ninety prisoners and advanced nearly a mile. They did not give up and they did not retreat from the fight as the 2nd and 3rd battalions had, but they had already lost a lot of men and were still more than three miles from breaking through to the Lost Battalion.

While I Company was holding its ground against German counterattacks, Lt. Marty Higgins of the Lost Battalion radioed division headquarters requesting bandages, sulfadiazine, and tape for casualties, and reported that another man had just died. Headquarters came up with another plan to supply the Lost Battalion and communicated it to Higgins. The idea was to fire supplies with artillery into the area by removing the chemical loads from M84 smoke shells and filling them with D-rations, medicine, and other provisions. The fuses were timed to burst 200 feet in the air, but while the Lost Battalion men could hear the shells overhead, by that time it was too dark to retrieve the contents. The decision was made to attempt an airdrop the next day.

Kash finally made his way back to the aid station and was anxious to get patched up quickly and back to the action with his men. As he looked around, he saw men with far more critical wounds than his and realized they had far more need for urgent care. The good news for Kash was that the medics didn't consider him to be a critical case, but the bad news was that Kash had to patiently await his turn, so he passed the time by talking with the others to learn what was going on in other parts of the battle. He also took some time to write to Louise on Red Cross stationery. Kash wrote Louise:

Part of a letter Kash wrote to Louise describing
the battles in the Vosges Forest of France

"I like to describe this war a little to you (in) just a few sentence(s). The weather is similar to Seattle rains like "H" and definitely cold. We sleep in slit trenches full of water, if you know what trench foot is, well a lot of the boys have it. The supply is hard to get and food sometimes does not come every day. Since we're fighting in forest mountains the shells bursts in the tree and the fragments really tears the boys apart. It's really a lovely picture, words cannot express this terrific thing called war. Well, I better change the subject. The reason I speak of this is because that's all I've seen and that's all I'll be seeing till this mess is over."

When his turn finally came, Kash told the medics to do the minimum required to get him back on the battlefield as fast as possible. After they examined his back, they removed the shrapnel, patched him up, gave him morphine to kill the pain, and recommended that he sit out the rest of the battle. But Kash had other ideas, none of which involved sitting out the battle. Despite orders to rest, Kash insisted that he needed to get back to the front, picked up his gear, and again left before anyone could stop him.

As the day turned to night, the rain continued to fall, and the retreating light of twilight once again turned to pitch black. Navigating the terrain at night was dangerous because the enemy was all around, and stumbling into a German machine gun nest could have deadly consequences. Movement at night was limited to only what was required, so the men dug in and covered themselves up as best they could with tree branches to protect themselves from tree bursts.

Perhaps it was the combination of morphine and adrenaline that kept Kash moving forward as if he never got injured as he found his way back to his men on the front lines. He moved from man to man, making sure everyone was okay and in the right positions. Nobody could understand how he was able to get around in the pitch darkness, and sometimes his men were startled by his sudden appearance. Whatever was driving Kash was somehow helping him see in the black of night. Maybe it was his color blindness, which is known to help with night vision, or maybe his burning determination to win the battle and prove his loyalty. Whatever the case, it seemed like nothing was going to stop him.

Whenever he could, he advanced his squad silently in the darkness until the risk of literally bumping into the enemy became too great. Then they hunkered down as best they could and waited for the next opportunity to continue moving forward. Injured and dying men—both American and German—could be heard calling out to their mothers. It broke every man's heart to hear one of their own calling out to his mother in Japanese, "Okaasan," until his voice eventually faded into silence. It was the kind of tragedy and experience that would repeat itself and haunt them for the rest of their lives. Throughout the night, the Germans intermittently fired tree bursts in their efforts to exhaust the men of the 442nd.

Battle of the Lost Battalion: Day Two, Saturday, October 28, 1944

Fear, cold, and the lack of sleep in the Vosges Forest placed enormous stresses on the men of the 442nd. The fog hovering over the forest offered both cover and an unsettling eeriness. The morning brought a continuation of the battle of the night before with the men dug in, desperate to survive. Some soldiers woke up to see bloodied bodies of their friends hit by tree bursts the night before.

The Lost Battalion prepared for the long-awaited airdrop. The weather was clear, and the Lost Battalion men tried to signal the planes with smoke grenades. But the planes overflew them, and Higgins reported back that the supplies had fallen into enemy hands.

Shortly after the failed airdrop, the 36th Division artillery, at last, began lofting supply shells to the Lost Battalion. The initial volleys were smoke shells to fix the range. Once they fixed in on the right range, the supply shells burst over the Lost Battalion, with the contents spilling down through the trees, scattering all over the area. Other shells plowed into the ground. The men scrambled to recover what they could. It was the first material proof in five days that relief was close at hand. They took stock of the supplies the men had recovered from the artillery shells, which gave them a sense of guarded optimism. Higgins radioed, "Received only rations. Have not found everything as yet. Have water. Hope to see friends tomorrow."

Surrounded by landmines and enemy fire, the men of 442nd advanced from tree to tree toward the Lost Battalion. Kash, having gotten patched up from the aid station the night before, moved from man to man, pushing his men forward as the enemy continued to fire on them along the way. Suddenly, the Germans unleashed the worst barrage of the battle as shells seemed to come in like machine gun bullets. It was a ferocious uphill battle, with tree bursts exploding overhead with deadly accuracy. Digging in for protection continued to be an exercise in futility as bombs exploded in the trees. But still the 442nd advanced. They fought up the mountainous terrain from tree to tree and bush to bush. They strained to see through the thick terrain so they could kill the enemy before the enemy killed them.

By that time, many more men of the 442nd suffered from trench foot, making it excruciatingly painful to move around. They tried as best they could to keep their feet dry, but the mud, rain, and an enemy bent on killing them made it impossible. The day continued as it had the previous day, with the 442nd continuing to advance, but every man knew that every step could be their last as the Germans made sure they paid a heavy price for every inch of ground they took.

Painting of "The 442nd Rescue of the Lost Battalion in Vosges, France" by Charles McBarrow. Courtesy of the Army Art Collection, U.S. Center of Military History

7

More Lost than Saved

It happened on the night of October 28, 1944. As the battle wore on, provisions became a problem for the 442nd. The men were beyond exhausted, and supplies were running low. That evening, as supply trucks were coming up from the rear, Battalion Commander Lt. Colonel A. Pursell gave the order for a detail of twelve volunteers led by Kash to meet the supply convoy and carry supplies back to the battlefield.

Heavy rain and slick roads were making it difficult for the supply trucks to reach the 442nd, who had just driven the Germans out of the area where the supply trucks were headed. Kash would later say that "It was so quiet that night you could hear a pin drop."

As the sound of the approaching supply trucks got closer, Lt. Colonel Pursell ordered the detail of volunteers to move down the hill immediately to meet the convoy, but Kash told Pursell that the Germans could hear the supply trucks and would barrage the exact route the men and vehicles would use since they had just moved out of the area hours before. He urged Pursell to hold off until morning, but Pursell insisted that they move out immediately. Despite orders to move out, Kash brought the men together and suggested that they hold off for a while, but some of the men said that when the Battalion Commander gives an order, they should follow it. So Kash quietly led the unprotected group of soldiers down the trail to the road where the trucks were pulling up.

Just as Kash had predicted, about 200 yards from where they started, the Germans launched an artillery barrage with pinpoint accuracy right on top of them. Exploding bombs lit up the whole area with thunderous explosions and flames that engulfed and illuminated the entire area. It was all but an inescapable kill zone with nowhere to hide. Bombs were exploding everywhere around them and in every direction on the ground and in the trees. Eight of the twelve men were blown up and killed instantly, and three were injured. Because the Germans knew the area and had pinpointed the trail, the attack on the twelve-man detail was a bloodbath. Miraculously, Kash was the only one who wasn't seriously injured in the barrage. He found one of the men, Kenneth Inada, who was unconscious and whose leg was nearly blown off. He hoisted Inada over his shoulder as the barrage of artillery continued and carried him back to the aid station. He went back to the kill zone to bring the rest of the wounded back to the aid station. The attack was devastating. Kash was so angry that he could not control his rage. He knew the Germans would hit them and that they should have waited, but Pursell's order gave them no choice.

When Kash returned to battalion command, he confronted Lt. Colonel Pursell and told him in no uncertain terms what he thought of Pursell and his order, and said that the men would rather have starved than suffer the casualties that occurred. Kash knew that some of the men who were killed came from Japanese American internment camps where their families had already lost so much, and that such a tragedy could have been averted. But that was no way for a Staff Sergeant to speak to a Battalion Commander. One of the men of the 442nd, Shig Doi, would later report overhearing Pursell telling his aids that Kash would pay for his insubordination. It was an encounter that would haunt Kash for the rest of his life.

Battle of the Lost Battalion: Day 3, October 29, 1944

The men of the Lost Battalion remained hopeful and courageous. Trapped for a week under intense pressure, rising casualties, and the pounding of artillery, the soldiers stood their ground. They did not move around during the daytime, and only got water at night under the cover of darkness at the same watering hole the Germans were using. They were ordered not to kill Germans at the watering hole for fear of contaminating the water with dead bodies. While remaining hopeful, the men of the Lost Battalion knew that their chances of coming out of there alive were practically non-existent unless somebody broke through.

For the most part, the Germans were directing their firepower downhill to repel the 442nd, rather than back at the Lost Battalion. But German harassing fire and snipers continued to take their toll on the Lost Battalion. As Higgins made his morning rounds of the perimeter, he found more corpses of American soldiers. With no graves registration unit to enter the dead, he radioed headquarters for advice on what to do to give them the respect they deserved and was told that unless and until they could be carried freely off the hill, the dead would have to lie where they fell—a lost battalion of souls. When the sky finally cleared above, the Lost Battalion's prayers were answered as supplies floated down above them by parachute from Allied aircraft, and the eager men below scrambled to retrieve the much-needed food, ammunition, and medicine before the Germans could get to them.

The men of the 442nd continued fighting against more artillery barrages, tree bursts, and machine gun fire. Regrouping in the mist, they readied themselves for the third day of their rescue mission, and what would be their greatest test as soldiers.

As the 442nd advanced, trench foot continued to set in for many of the men, and the artillery barrages intensified. Back from the aid station and his harrowing supply run, Shiro led his men, moving from

This is a modern-day photo of one of the areas where the Lost Battalion dug in and fought to survive after being surrounded by the Germans. Photo courtesy of the author, John Suzuki.

man-to-man avoiding small arms fire and tree bursts. They continued to move forward tree by tree as the enemy fired directly at wave after wave of attacking troops of the 442nd, killing and wounding many.

As the battle continued, German artillery fired a concentrated barrage on the 442nd and the men took cover as best they could. Because they had advanced into the German lines, they were able to take cover in deep fox holes and machine gun nests previously made by the Germans. In some cases, dead Germans still occupied the foxholes, the stench of which was so bad that they were immediately abandoned for different cover. But even with the added cover of the previously German placements, the tree bursts were so effective that heavy casualties continued to ensue as the 442nd continued their advance.

The farther the 442nd advanced, the more confusing the battle became. The Germans were so scattered that sometimes they were twenty feet away, and sometimes they were behind the advancing Japanese Americans. In the midst of the confusion, many men on both sides were cut down by machine gun fire.

Both sides were so closely positioned to each other in the jungle-like terrain that American artillery spotters were unable to clearly distinguish German positions from American positions. Air support was rendered ineffective for the same reasons. As for American tanks, the rain and mud made it nearly impossible for the tanks to navigate. It all came down to lone men making the most difficult choices under the most extreme circumstances. Without the support of air power, armor, or artillery, the men of the 442nd knew their fate was literally in their own hands, and it all led to what would later be called an "almost suicidal" assault.

The more the 442nd advanced toward the Lost Battalion, the more desperately the enemy fought. Despite the close-in fighting, German artillery continued to fire as tree bursts exploded atop both American and German positions. They were firing their artillery indiscriminately, without concern of killing their own forces. The Germans suddenly became as fearful of their own artillery as the Americans were. Men on both sides were being killed and injured by the tree bursts. It was the fiercest fighting of the battle thus far.

As Kash scouted the hill that separated them from the Lost Battalion, he saw men on his left catch a barrage and suddenly disappeared from view of his men. He ran back to tell the group to move to their right to avoid the shelling. He knew there were two machine gun nests in front of him, and they had to be taken out. Kash's own men had no idea where he went, but they all knew that Kash always took the most dangerous assignments himself and suspected he moved forward by himself to scout more of the enemy positions ahead. Moments later, German gunfire rang out and nobody knew who or what they were shooting at. Suddenly, as Kash came running back down the hill to his men, one of the German bullets hit Kash in the back. When he reached his platoon, he reported the number of Germans and their positions on the other side of the hill.

Ignoring his gunshot wound, Kash prepared for the desperate battle on what would later be called "Suicide Hill." I Company was pinned down and could not move. Readying themselves for the assault, Kash and his men fixed their bayonets to their rifles. Kash needed to find Barney Hajiro, the soldier booted out of M Company for being a troublemaker, who carried a light machine gun—a Browning Automatic Rifle or BAR. Hajiro had taken cover with his assistant, Takeyasu Onaga, and was doing a final check on his automatic weapon when Kash suddenly crashed into their foxhole and crawled over to join them.

As Kash briefed Hajiro on the German positions, Hajiro noticed that Kash's face looked flush and that he didn't look so good. Kash mentioned that he had been shot in the shoulder and insisted that he was fine, but Hajiro convinced him to get his wound treated and stitched up. Hajiro would later say, "Here I am, a buck private telling a staff sergeant what to do. I thought maybe I was going to get kicked out again."

It didn't take long for Kash to begrudgingly agree to get patched up again, and told Hajiro and Onaga that he would be back. So once again, with every intention to return to the battle, Kash disengaged and headed back to the aid station.

Staying covered and being as careful as he could, Hajiro saw his buddies being picked off by machine gun and sniper fire, and he knew that someone had to act since there were no officers left standing. The BAR provided the firepower to lead the attack, but he knew it would also make him the prime target of the enemy. But Barney Hajiro, a buck private, knew he had to neutralize the enemy to prevent more casualties. He gathered extra ammo, hefted his BAR, and suddenly stood up. He launched a banzai charge and took off shouting and yelling at the top of his lungs, advancing from tree to tree and concentrating his fire at a machine gun nest. During the charge, he confronted a tank and yelled for a bazooka. Onaga came running down the hill with his bazooka and was hit. Grasping his neck to stop the blood, the medic told him to lie down, but seconds later, Onaga was dead.

Seeing Onaga die enraged Hajiro. He continued to advance alone against heavy German fire. The other men of the 442nd saw Hajiro drawing heavy German fire and rose to their feet, charging and falling in great numbers. The carnage was so intense that the area would later be called "Suicide Hill." German machine guns rained fire on the men wherever they moved. "You God-damn Jerries!" Hajiro swore as he rushed forward. "You fucking buggahs!"

A soldier of the 442d advances upwards against German resistance. With the Germans dug in, camouflaged, and holding the high ground, the fighting was deadly and intense. Photo courtesy of the National Archives and Records Administration.

Halfway up the 100-yard slope, he opened fire at twenty yards and killed three Germans in a machine gun nest. He then saw other fellow soldiers moving forward, also firing and attacking with crazed-like shouts. Battered and bloodied men were all around, yet they kept gaining ground; rallying, relying on one another, and advancing even as buddies cried out "Mama!" before dying, assaulting the enemy stronghold. A German machine gunner fired at Hajiro and missed. Hajiro pinned the enemy crew down with a blast and fired again. Two more Germans died. He encountered a sniper guarding a machine gun nest. He fired his BAR and killed the German.

Hajiro stumbled upon another enemy machine gun, but this time, Hajiro's breathtaking advance between oncoming bullets came to a brutal halt. Four bullets riddled his arm and pierced his side. His helmet went flying and his BAR shattered. As Hajiro fell, the men of the 442nd shouted at the enemy and fired their weapons with raging fury and hurled themselves at the remaining Germans, at first blazing away point blank, then rushing in with bayonets and grenades, and finally engaging in savage hand-to-hand combat.

Disengaging from the battle, Hajiro walked down "Suicide Hill," bleeding all the way. Perhaps by mercy or simple luck, Hajiro would later say that the Germans gave him a break, since no one shot at him as he made his way back to safety. Although he was seriously wounded, he insisted that the other wounded men be treated before him. When asked why he took the actions he did, Hajiro would later say that he didn't think about dying, and that he knew that in battle, automatic weapons go first.

The remaining men of the 442nd continued to advance. At that point of the battle, most of the men of the 442nd had been killed or injured. The fighting was as fierce as ever, but the 442nd continued to advance. There were so many men, both American and German, who were wounded or dead.

At the aid station, Kash got the medical attention he required after having been shot in the back and was told to rest. The bullet came within a fraction of an inch of hitting his spine. He was lucky. But again, he wanted to join his men in breaking through to the Lost Battalion, so again he ran away from the aid station before anyone could stop him. As he made his way back to the front, he was intercepted by Smitty Koga, who was driving a supply jeep. Smitty told Kash to get aboard for a ride back up to the fighting. As they drove up the road, they encountered some men of the 442nd and pulled over for the latest updates. After a few moments of talking, all the men suddenly dove under the jeep and yelled at each other to take cover. Not realizing what was happening, Kash laughed and asked what was going on. Just then, tree bursts exploded above them, raining down burning shrapnel and nearly ripping Kash's leg off. Kash hit the ground and took cover, but it was too late. His injury was too serious for him to go back to the fight, and he wasn't going anywhere. For Kash, the Battle of the Lost Battalion was over, and word spread that he may lose his leg and he was finally going home.

Later, as Kash was transported in an ambulance, he spoke to another injured soldier, Gilbert Kobatake, and was heartbroken to learn that his Captain, Joseph Byrne, had died that morning after having stepped on a Bouncing Betty landmine as he was trying to outflank the enemy. Captain Byrne was one of the 442nd's most respected officers who not only welcomed the assignment as a white officer in the all-Japanese American 442nd RCT, but made every effort to support and respect his men. Kash told Kobatake that he left the aid station the first time because of Captain Byrne. He was a good man.

Captain Byrne's death was a blow to all the men, but it meant the most to Shorty, who was Byrne's trusted runner. Shorty was recuperating in an Army hospital during the battle of the Lost Battalion. When Captain Byrne died, Shorty received a call from Major Emmet O'Connor to inform him personally of the captain's death. With Byrne being the tallest man of I Company and Shorty the shortest, many of the men referred to them as "Mutt and Jeff." At one point, Byrne sent Shorty on a ten-day leave to go to Italy for custom-made shoes. Shorty grew up in Hawaii wearing slippers and going barefoot, so his feet were wide and strong. The shoemakers of Italy made Shorty shoes that were size 2½, super wide. One of those pairs of shoes is in the Smithsonian. When Shorty rejoined the company, they gave him every honor of a man who had lost his father.

Battle of the Lost Battalion: Day 4, October 30, 1944

Headquarters ordered Higgins to be prepared to attack and to check in every fifteen minutes for further instructions. Higgins reported that German patrols were harassing their position. An hour later, Higgins reported that the situation was getting worse with active enemy patrols. Headquarters told Higgins to stay on alert, as the 442nd was at that point about one mile away.

With a relatively stable front established overnight, instead of the rapidly shifting battle lines from the previous day, American artillery was finally able to direct a heavy barrage in the area where the Germans were still placed separating the 442nd from the Lost Battalion. Following the bombardment, the cautiously advancing soldiers of the 442nd found large amounts of enemy clothing and supplies littered across the area just beyond Suicide Hill. Although all was quiet, they were weary of German snipers still concealed in the heavy brush. With their senses on high alert, they moved forward ever so deliberately, prepared to fire at anything that moved.

As the 442nd cautiously advanced, Henry Nakada moved forward at point with Mutt Sakumoto second and the rest of the company behind them. Sakumoto saw movement up ahead, but Nakada didn't see it. Sakumoto moved cautiously toward the area of the movement. Was it a German or someone from the Lost Battalion? His mind raced as he tried to identify friend from foe, since it could cost him his life if he guessed wrong.

On the other side of the hill, Sergeant Edward Guy of the Lost Battalion was on outpost when he saw somebody slowly approaching and aimed his rifle as he strained his eyes to see who it was. He was told that the 442nd was close, but was also wary of German troops still in the area. Trying hard to keep his heart from beating out of his chest and his breathing steady, he looked straight into Sakumoto's direction.

Finally, as their eyes met, they looked at each other until Sergeant Guy dropped his rifle and motioned to his buddies that the 442nd had arrived. Then he raced down the hill like a crazed madman, yelling, laughing, grabbing, and hugging Sakumoto. Surprised and not knowing what to say, the first thing Sakumoto could think of saying was "Do you guys need any cigarettes?"

As word quickly spread that they were finally rescued, every soldier of the Lost Battalion emerged from their positions with joy and relief that their saviors arrived. The other Japanese American men of the 442nd cautiously followed Sakumoto, watching him for the "all clear" signal. When he finally gave the signal, they moved forward with relief, knowing that they had won the battle.

To the men of the 442nd, finally seeing the men of the Lost Battalion was an unbelievable sight. 211 men of the Lost Battalion eventually came out of their foxholes; their gaunt faces expressing relief and gratitude. Everyone was elated. Dropping their weapons they ran and hugged each other saying "God, thank you, thank you, thank you."

The meeting of the Japanese Americans with the Lost Battalion was a touching moment, writes Chaplain Masao Yamada. "They smiled heartily at the Japanese Americans and for a moment forgot the ugliness of war." Many shook hands and said, "If it weren't for you, only God knows what would have happened to us."

But the 442nd could not stop for long, as they were given orders to continue past the Lost Battalion and advance to the next hill. The Lost Battalion of the famed Alamo Regiment was saved by the Japanese American 442nd Regimental Combat Team in a victory that would later be recognized as one of the ten greatest battles in American history.

On November 12, 1944, Shiro wrote Louise a V-MAIL that read:

Dear Lou,

Well, I have sort of a rugged story to tell you. I guess you received my last V-Mail mentioning my being hit in the back. Well, I went to the hospital on the day I got hit. The wound was slight, and you know the hot head I am, so I insisted that I go back up to the front. So I started up and I certainly didn't get far cuz a shell landed right next to me. Well, anyway, I was lucky just to get a piece of lead in my leg. They operated on my leg and removed the lead, so I'll be o.k. I'll probably be in the hospital a month or so. I guess my luck ran out on me cuz it's the third injury I received here. Let's hope they stay just minor injuries. Well, take care of yourself and keep your chin up. I'll try to come home in one piece.

Love, Shiro

On November 12, General Dahlquist ordered the 442nd Regimental Combat Team to pass in review, where all the men of the 442nd were to line up in formation and parade in unison for the General to review and congratulate. What was expected to be several thousand men of three battalions and headquarters instead ended up being a few hundred; the equivalent of significantly less than one battalion.

When the General saw the absence of so many men, he openly reprimanded his officers saying that "When I order everyone to pass in review, I mean the cooks and everybody will pass in review."

Chaplain Yamada quietly explained to the General that the men who stood before him were all that was left of the 442nd Regimental Combat Team, and that the rest had been killed or injured. The General knew that many of their families were incarcerated in internment camps, but until that moment he did not realize how many men were lost.

While the battle of the Lost Battalion was won by the 442nd RCT, who succeeded where no other soldiers could, their losses were enormous, with over 800 dead and wounded, saving just 211. It was later determined that of the estimated 150 men of I Company who started in the battle, only eight walked off the battlefield. But despite sustaining more casualties than men saved of the Lost Battalion, the men of the 442nd knew they did their jobs and proved their courage and loyalty to the United States of America.

At the end of the battles in France, the 442nd had lost so many men and was so depleted that the regiment was sent to southern France to spend the final winter of World War II defending the French-Italian border as fresh reinforcements arrived to bring the 442nd back to full strength. Kash, in the meantime, was sent to England to recover from his wounds, which many thought would mean the amputation of his leg. But the doctors were fortunately able to save Kash's leg, which took three months of recovery. He spent much of his time writing to Louise, who faithfully wrote back to him as often as she could. He would often entertain the other men by reading Louise's letters to them, which everyone enjoyed and appreciated.

Dear Lou,

How's my honey getting along with all those wolves back in Chicago? Well, I guess I'm cooped up for a month or so in a hospital, so I guess you don't have to worry about me. Boy, it's tough staying in bed when you're not used to it, gads, it's no fun. By the way, I saw my wound yesterday and it's a hole about the size of my fist. It's sure lucky the shrapnel never hit my bone, or maybe I'd be on a boat home. That bullet wound in my back, if a little closer, would have hit my spine and I would be in (a) markless field, see how lucky I was. The only way I'll probably die is of liquor, no kidding.

I got one complaint to make about the hospital. Well, I guess it's not their fault. Well, it's that bed pan. I don't care how long I'll be laid up, I certainly won't get used to that thing. Words cannot express its morale breaking ability.

Well, I guess I better change the subject. When I get to the general hospital I'll write to you every day. Don't worry about me. I'm always okay.

Love, Shiro

Louise would be visited in Chicago by many of Kash's friends who had been discharged from the Army and were on their way home, some of whom would tell her that Kash was finally coming home due to his injuries. But Kash never let on to how truly serious his injuries were and chalked it up as no big deal. Still, Louise kept her hopes up that Kash would come home, though she also knew that he would stay and fight for as long as he was allowed. His place was with his men, and he would not leave them as long as he had a fighting breath left in him.

During his recovery, Kash ran into other injured men of the 442nd, which helped to keep him from going crazy as he recovered. Being happy-go-lucky and friendly to everyone, it was easy for him to make friends with the hospital staff and fellow patients. He always enjoyed hearing stories about other men's experiences and was a great student of battlefield tactics. He realized that everything he learned could help keep his men alive and lead them to victory when he got back to the business of war.

When Kash's leg wound had finally healed, he was told by an officer that he could head home. He had suffered what was called "a million-dollar wound," and the Army was letting him go home if he wanted to. Kash knew that Louise was anxiously awaiting his return and his heart ached to see her again. But he also believed that Louise would understand his need to stay with his men to see the war through, as it would be his greatest regret if he went home and harm came to any of his men. Rejecting the opportunity to go home, he requested to be reinstated to active duty, and to be assigned back to the 442nd.

Kash's request to be reinstated was granted and he was ordered to escort several soldiers across the English Channel to be reassigned in France, where he would be given his new orders away from the 442nd. Desperately wanting to rejoin his men who were now in southern France, Kash decided to take his chances. After he completed his assignment, he asked around to find out where the 442nd was deployed. Hearing that they had moved to southern France, he took off to rejoin the 442nd in a small French town just outside of Monaco.

8

Incarcerated Again

Kash was ecstatic when he finally caught up to the 442nd in the little town of Beausoleil just outside Monaco. As he walked around trying to find his platoon, everyone was stunned to see him walking on two legs, let alone back in action. Many of the men were told that Kash was going to lose his leg and he was going home. Now, three and a half months later, Kash showed up in Southern France as if nothing happened. All the men were happy to see him but could not believe that he had chosen to stay and fight instead of going home to Louise after all he had been through.

That night, Kash asked George Morihiro what they were doing and was disgusted to hear that they were just going to hang out and play cards. As far as Kash was concerned, he figured they could all be dead the next day, so he told Morihiro that they should all go out and enjoy themselves. To add a little spirit into the mix, it was Valentine's Day, so he thought it might be fun to score a dance or two. Not wanting to disappoint Kash, all the men skipped their card game and went out on the town, having no idea of the trouble that awaited them that evening, February 14, 1945.

It started out innocently enough with some drinking and dancing in a dance hall called Dancing Augeste. Kash, Sergeant Fred Matsumura, Beanie Hayashi, and a few others were relaxing and drinking beer at a long table when a group of Military Police officers arrived. Sensing that something was wrong, Matsumura got up to ask if everything was okay. When the MP asked him if the belligerent guy at the bar was one of his men, Matsumura acknowledged that the guy was his, and the MP told him to take care of him because he was drunk and disorderly. Assuring the MP that he would take care of him, the MPs started to leave the dance hall and Matsumura went back to the table with Kash and Hayashi. Moments later, a scuffle broke out. For whatever reason, the drunk guy, Private First Class James Matsuda, punched one of the MP officers and all hell broke loose.

Nobody seemed to know who did what and why everyone was fighting, but what started with a single punch ended up becoming a barroom brawl. Finally, Kash, Matsumura, and Hayashi went in and were able to break up the men who were fighting. With the three men's intervention, the misunderstanding was amicably settled with 1st Lt. Jorge Suro, Jr., the ranking officer who got punched. When things settled down, he decided not to press charges or arrest anyone, ordered everyone to go back to their respective quarters and called it a night.

The next morning started just like any other Thursday morning. Kash was talking with Beanie about what had happened the night before and how fortunate Matsuda was that he didn't get arrested for punching the MP officer. Suddenly, "a whole slew" of MPs showed up with orders to round up the ten soldiers who were at the dance hall the previous night. Confused as to why they were now being arrested after having been released with no charges filed, Kash asked to see Lt. Jorge Suro, the MP officer who had been punched, to understand why they were now being arrested. But Lt. Suro was not present. Instead, the arresting officer in charge that morning was none other than Lt. Colonel Pursell himself, the same Lt. Colonel who Kash insubordinately chewed out for his misguided order to bring up supplies during the Battle of the Lost Battalion that resulted in the deaths of eight men and three wounded.

While none of the men knew why they were being arrested, Kash figured that once they spoke to Lt. Suro and realized it was only one man, PFC James Matsuda, who punched the MP officer, the rest of the men would be released. But later that day when they released everyone except Kash, Beanie, Fred Matsumura, and James Matsuda, and ordered them into the stockade (military prison) to await court-martial, Kash knew exactly what was happening; Lt. Colonel Pursell was getting his revenge.

Everyone knew that Matsuda was the one who caused all the trouble, but Matsuda would not confess, and none of the other men would betray their honor by snitching on him. So, the 442nd RTC Chaplain, Masao Yamada, and Lieutenant S. Kubota visited Matsuda and asked him to admit that he caused the trouble so the others could go free, but he refused. Two days later, Chaplain Yamada said that Lt. Colonel Pursell intended to make an example of the men who were involved in the bar room incident. The chaplain also said that the MP officer, Lt. Suro, confirmed that Matsuda was the primary and only cause of the incident, and had requested directly to Lt. Colonel Pursell that all charges against the four men be dropped. Lt. Suro also learned that Matsumura, Kashino, and Hayashi had refrained from implicating Matsuda. The four men continued to be confined despite the MP officer's request that the charges be dropped and remained jailed in the stockade. Kash wrote to Louise with the bad news.

> *I got a little bad news for you and I hope you won't take it too bad. Well, anyway, I got into trouble last week on Valentine's Day. I took off from camp with a few boys and I got drunk and got into some trouble. I guess we got mixed up with some MPs and we've been in jail since. Well, I told you before as soon as I was off the line I won't hold the stripes. I sure made a mess of it, but don't worry, I can still take it...*

Life in the stockade turned out to be perfectly fine with Kash, though they were often ordered to repeatedly dig and fill up six by six-foot holes just to humiliate them. When Kash, Beanie, and Fred were guarded by other men of the 442nd, they were able to invite bunches of buddies who would bring beer and hang out with them.

Sometimes they would have as many as fifteen men drinking beer and playing cards. And when they would occasionally want to go into town, the "guards" would turn the other way and they'd go into town. Nobody really cared as long as they stayed out of trouble, and everyone did their part to make the best of a bad situation.

About a month later, in mid-March, the 442nd received their orders to head back to Italy as Kash, Matsumura, and Beanie were still being held in the stockade for a crime they didn't commit and were never charged for. When word got to them that the 442nd was moving out the following day, Kash was disappointed to miss out on the coming battle and wanted to fight alongside his men. After all, this was the reason why he came back to the 442nd instead of going home when he nearly lost his leg. But he resigned himself to being stuck in the stockade and not being allowed to fight. Inexplicably, hours before the 442nd moved out, Lt. Colonel Pursell ordered Kash and the other three men to be released from the stockade and assigned back to I Company to help lead their men in an upcoming battle in Italy. Pursell knew that their leadership was needed, since most of the experienced leaders were either killed or wounded in previous battles.

They were ecstatic to be released since it meant they were now free men, and they hurried back to rejoin their men. Arriving back to where I Company was preparing to deploy, everyone was happy to have Kash back to lead them into battle. Even the replacement soldiers who were brought in to bring the 442nd back to full strength, while somewhat intimidated by Kash's reputation as a tough and gutsy soldier, were happy to have Kash as their leader. Matsumura would later recount Kash always wanting to move forward, saying, "Come on, let's go get 'em!"

Matsumura would always try to get Kash to be more careful and deliberate, telling him to slow down, but Kash would always insist, "No, come on, let's go, let's go!!" Now they were being called back to fight what was to be another epic battle of World War II; the Battle of the Gothic Line.

9

The Impossible Mission

Spanning across Italy from west to east is the Apennine Mountain Range, also known as the Gothic Line. Throughout the history of warfare, no army that held the tops of this mountain range was ever dislodged by enemy forces. The Gothic Line was the final major German defensive line in northern Italy, which stretched across Italy from Massa on the west coast to the area near Pesaro on the east coast. Access was limited to a handful of known roads and trails that were heavily guarded and fortified by the Germans. It was a formidable barrier that proved itself to be virtually impenetrable against attacking forces for centuries.

By March 1945, General Mark Clark's 5th Army, along with other Allied forces, had tried unsuccessfully for six months to overtake the western end of the Gothic Line near Massa, Italy. It was theorized that once the western end was taken, the Allies could move east atop the Apennine Mountains, defeating the Germans all the way to the eastern shores of Italy. But the Germans also knew the strategic importance and had built their defenses fortified with tons of steel and stone. The Germans forced an estimated 10,000 Italians into hard labor to make over 2,500 machine gun nests and concrete bunkers, some of which were built into the mountains themselves providing natural protection and rendering Allied artillery ineffective. The main defense for the Germans was the mountain range itself. With inclines at sixty degrees and higher, and over 3,000 feet high, much of the

Gothic Line was more like a series of cliffs than a mountain range. And attacking the Germans up the main access roads and trails at the front of the mountain range proved to be not only futile, but fatal, since the Germans had virtually every inch covered with machine guns and artillery. Even though displacing the army holding the Gothic Line had never been accomplished in the history of warfare, General Clark had attempted every option he had available to him, but the Germans repelled every attack thrown at them.

With the 442nd back to full strength, General Clark ordered them back to the 92nd Infantry Division of the 5th Army in Italy, which they had left six months prior to fight in the battles of Bruyeres and the Lost Battalion. Victory at the Gothic Line was an imperative for the Allies to achieve victory in Italy and continue their march into Germany, and the 442nd had proven themselves to be an indomitable fighting force with a perfect battle record. Having exhausted all his resources and options over six months, General Clark was now calling on the 442nd to join the fight.

Realizing that none of the previous strategies of the 5th Army were successful, the commanders of the 442nd RCT knew they had to come up with a battle strategy that nobody had thought of over the centuries of warfare at the Gothic Line. After careful analysis and conferring amongst themselves, the leaders of the 442nd presented a plan to General Clark and his commanders that had indeed never been considered before. It was crazy, brazen, and outrageous to suggest that what the entire 5th Army couldn't accomplish in six months, the 442nd would accomplish in forty-eight hours. Some said it was impossible. Some even scoffed at the idea. But it was the plan that the commanders of the 442nd were committed to.

The plan was bold and simple: with the Germans guarding every inch of *known* access points of the Gothic Line, including roads and trails, the 442nd proposed attacking the Germans from *unknown* access points. Specifically, to do something that had never been done in any prior battle of the Gothic Line; attack them from the *back* cliffside of the mountains and overtake and secure the western end of the Gothic Line near and including Monte Folgorito, which towered above the town of Massa on the western coast of Italy. Some thought it was a plan doomed to failure from the start.

Being a virtual cliff at a sixty-plus-degree incline, the only way up the backside of the Gothic Line was by using goat trails. The problem was that the men were neither goats nor nearly as surefooted as goats, so the question became one of figuring out how to get 5,000 men with heavy gear and fighting equipment up a 3,000-foot virtual cliff using goat trails in the dark of night without being detected by the enemy. Further complicating matters was the fact that the Germans could see everything happening around them for twenty miles from their lookouts atop the Gothic Line.

The plan hatched by the 442nd was kept in complete secrecy. It involved two days of hiding and two nights of marching first to the tiny town of Azzano, which was across a valley directly facing the back side of the Gothic Line in direct eyeshot of German sentries. To avoid detection by the Germans, they were to march in complete silence and the pitch-dark cover of night for ten hours along a dry riverbed and climb up a 1,000-foot embankment to Azzano before daybreak with orders not to cry out if they fell.

The 442nd was to remain hidden and silent during the day in Azzano until nightfall, at which time they were to climb back down 1,000 feet to the riverbed below, cross to the other side, and climb up the 3,000-foot cliff in pitch darkness, again with orders not to cry out if they fell. They were to reach the top by daybreak to begin their attack, and it was all predicated on the hope that the Germans were not guarding the back side of the Gothic Line. That was the theory, and it was utter madness. The 442nd was once again being called in to do what nobody else could do, including the entire 5th Army of the United States.

Battle of the Gothic Line: April 3, 1945

From ten miles away, 5,000 men of the 442nd moved out in the dark of night and complete silence toward the town of Azzano. Every possible precaution was taken to noise-proof everything that could make any kind of sound. Anything that clinked or clicked was silenced and secured, and the men were ordered not to talk or make any noise whatsoever. For nearly ten hours they marched in complete silence to Azzano. The march was grueling, as they had to navigate in complete darkness across an uneven and rocky riverbed, and then climb 1,000 feet up the side of the valley to Azzano without being detected by the Germans. Every man knew that any detection of the 442nd's presence would doom the entire mission. Not a word was spoken, and they moved with phantom-like silence. They made not a sound except for their quiet footsteps and occasional branch breaking under their weight. When they finally reached Azzano after their ten-mile march and 1,000-foot climb, all of the men quickly and quietly dispersed into and around the buildings and houses in the tiny village. Their job was to be invisible.

As the sun came up marking a new day, the men of the 442nd stayed completely covered up and concealed to avoid German detection. The men rested and slept as much as their adrenaline-pumped minds and bodies would allow for the coming battle, and they remained stone cold silent. No playing cards, no talking; no noise was allowed. There were many more Japanese American soldiers than residents in the tiny town that day. They stayed in barns, houses, and supply shacks. Kash and Beanie slept in a room with the sunlight blacked out. When they woke up, the wife gave them sausage soup, which they ate with gusto. They were so grateful for her kindness and nourishment. For the entire day they stayed completely concealed and silent until nightfall.

As darkness fell, Kash checked on his men in complete silence as they began their final preparations for their assault on the Gothic Line. Their equipment and weapons were checked and double checked to make certain nothing made any noise. As was the case the night before during their march and climb to Azzano, their final order was to fall in silence and not cry out, since any kind of sound could have betrayed the regiment and resulted in total disaster. Chaplain Yamada was with the men and maintained his silence as he ministered to them before they moved out. They silently placed their palms together in prayer and secured their backpacks, weapons, and gear as they headed out.

Unlike the Battle of the Lost Battalion, where they went into the battle tired, exhausted, and depleted from the battle of Bruyeres in France just a day prior, all of the men were now rested and ready to go. Kash, Fred Matsumura, and Beanie were happy with having been released from the stockade and were ready to help lead the men to victory on the Gothic Line, which everyone understood also meant victory in Italy and an open path for the Allies' final push into Germany.

2nd Lt. Daniel Inouye was also checking on his men to prepare for the battle. He had previously been called back to battalion headquarters the day before the battle of the Lost Battalion to be given a field commission to 2nd Lieutenant and was unable to get back to the 442nd until after the Lost Battalion had been rescued. He recalled being worried when he was called to battalion headquarters and thought he was in trouble for organizing poker games in the 442nd. Inouye knew that the house made the most money, and being the house for the 442nd was no exception. He made a lot of money. But instead of busting him for gambling, the battalion brass gave him a battlefield commission to 2nd Lieutenant. He could not believe his luck.

2nd Lt. Inouye was ready to lead his men to victory. He recalled the words of his father, *"Never shame America and your family."* They were as clear in his mind as the day his dad had spoken them. Now he was about to lead his men into one of the most dangerous and epic battles of World War II.

Modern day view of the (western) backside of the Gothic Line from the town of Azzano. Note Monte Folgorito, the westernmost peak of the Gothic Line on the left. Photo courtesy of Davide del Giudice.

Modern day view of Azzano from atop the Gothic Line.

The 442nd moved out at 2000 hours (8:00 p.m.) in pitch darkness and absolute silence. There was no parade, no fanfare; just dead silence. As they left the town of Azzano, they worked their way down 1,000 feet to the valley floor and marched along and across the dry riverbed on the valley floor to the designated point where they were to begin their 3,000-foot climb to the top of the western end of the Gothic Line. Every man had the same thing on their minds—if you fall, do not make a sound. Cover your mouth if you have to. The paths they took were so narrow that they were forced to climb single file, one man at a time. The goat trails were marked with white paper left by brave Italian partisans who had scouted out the trail just days prior. Now the entire regiment was being led up those trails by those same brave men.

One by one, the men began their epic climb, each with full packs, weapons, and the knowledge that a single slip or mistake could kill them and everyone else. Each held onto a strap on the pack of the man ahead of him since it was so difficult to see. When they reached 1,000 feet, one of the men stopped and was unable to move. He was frozen in fear. As the men behind him encouraged him to keep moving, he was unable to move. So, to keep moving forward, the men had to leapfrog over him. About 1,500 feet up, one of the men lost his footing and fell. Terrified, he covered his mouth as he fell and landed in a patch of rocks and bushes 100 feet below. Thankfully, he wasn't killed, but his injuries prevented him from fighting in this battle.

This was a climb that required more concentration than anything they had ever done, and the steepness was something they didn't train for at Camp Shelby. Although Kash would usually encourage his men to keep going, he could not make a sound, so all he could do was to go through the line as best he could, tapping the shoulders of the men with encouragement. Everyone trusted Kash and knew he would do his best to take care of them.

Eight hours into their climb, Kash and the men of I Company finally reached the top of the mountain ridge in an area known as the "Saddle." With their hearts pounding and adrenaline pumping, they pulled themselves over the top, ready to fight. But there were no alarms or alerts issued by the enemy; there was just complete silence. They had reached the top of the Gothic Line completely undetected. The men quietly fanned out to the right along the top of the ridge line, which gave them the advantage of starting their attack from the high ground. As they took their positions, they all realized that the Germans were still sleeping in their foxholes and bunkers.

Current day photo of the "Saddle" where I-Company summited the Gothic Line. Monte Folgorito and the western end of the Gothic Line can be seen in the far right background. Photo courtesy of the author, John Suzuki.

While the Germans were most certainly awake and actively guarding the front side of the mountains where the 5th Army had previously attacked, the Germans had never seen, nor expected, any threat coming from the back side of the mountain. So, while the 442nd knew that German guards were posted everywhere on the front side, the question was how much were they paying attention to the back side early in the morning. Now that the men had reached the top without being detected, the answer was clear: they weren't.

As Kash and his men quietly reached their positions, they did their best to conceal themselves, which was difficult to do since, unlike the Battle of the Lost Battalion, they were now at the top of a mountain where there were few trees and bushes. As they hunkered down into their positions to await orders to attack, the entire mountain range was completely quiet. All the men knew that within a few moments, the silence would be shattered with bombs, machine gun fire, blood, and terror as they fought for their lives and victory for America. And still the Germans slept.

As 2nd Lt. Daniel Inouye and his men reached the top, they fanned out and positioned themselves around a German bunker. Just then, the morning silence was broken as a German soldier sauntered out. The

Americans immediately ducked and hid. As the German moved about, he started to cook breakfast. Little did he know that his enemy was less than ten feet away from him and that his life, and that of every German in that bunker, would end in mere minutes. Daniel Inouye would later say that he felt bad for that cook.

When the order to attack was finally given, everyone attacked all at once. The Germans were completely surprised, and many of them were killed inside their bunkers before they could engage into the fight. The men of the 442nd moved forward as fast as they could to take advantage of the element of surprise, destroying every German who stood in the way or taking them prisoner as they advanced forward. Kash took the lead as he always did and led his men across the ridgetop at breathtaking speed. As he made his way forward shooting his Tommy gun and running up a hill, an enemy soldier jumped out of his fox hole and yelled as he threw a grenade. Kash ducked and fired his gun, killing the German, and kept moving forward. His men advanced with him and routed the enemy as the Germans desperately tried to counterattack.

The 442nd moved forward with stunning speed. German reinforcements that came up the main road were stopped in their tracks by I Company. As an entire column of about 200 Germans soldiers advanced up the main road, Kash and his men waited for them to reach a clearing of a granite rockfall where there were no trees and no cover. As the Germans reached the clearing in the road, Kash and his men opened fire, wiping them out.

2nd Lt. Inouye was leading his men, firing his Tommy gun and advancing toward machine gun nests. Moving forward undetected within a throw's distance, he pulled the pin of his grenade and threw it into a machine gun nest, then followed the explosion with his Tommy gun, wiping the Germans out. Seeing another machine gun nest ahead, he crawled forward without being detected. But as he prepared to take out the second nest, Inouye was hit in the stomach by a sniper's bullet and immediately hit the ground. His men saw him get hit and called for a medic, but Inouye waved them off, driven by determination to wipe out that second machine gun nest. He continued to crawl forward until he was in range to throw his hand grenade and wiped out that machine gun nest like he did the first.

Severely injured, Inouye continued moving forward. Spotting a third machine gun nest, he once again crawled toward it. When he came within range, he pulled the pin of his grenade and stood up to throw it. Just then, an enemy soldier popped up with a grenade rifle at point blank range and fired at Inouye, ripping through his right arm, leaving it dangling with his right hand still holding the live grenade. After prying it out with his left hand, he threw the grenade into the machine gun nest and followed the explosion again and destroyed the enemy with his Tommy gun. And still he led his men in advancing forward, refusing help from the medics.

When the battle ended and the area was secure, Inouye finally allowed the medics to tend to him. He had been shot twice and his right arm was beyond saving. It had to be amputated. The field hospital was several hours away, and he had to be carried since there was no way he could walk. As he was being carried by two prisoners, the German army counterattacked with artillery fire and the prisoners dropped Inouye to take cover. When the attack was over, everyone emerged from their cover. One of the men of the 442nd lined up the German prisoners and asked who was carrying 2nd Lt. Inouye. As the two identified themselves they were shot on the spot, and the two replacements were told that the same thing would happen to them if they dropped him as they resumed their trek to get Inouye the medical attention he required. As Daniel Inouye recalled, "You know, they never dropped me again after that."

Several hours later, they finally arrived at the field hospital, where Inouye was placed alongside other soldiers who were wounded in the battle. Looking around, he saw that all of the men around him had red marks on their foreheads and realized that he was placed with the men who were mortally wounded and being given their final rites. He was so severely injured that the field hospital personnel believed he was going to die. When the chaplain came to see him, Inouye told him that he wasn't ready to die yet and wasn't going anywhere. With haste, the chaplain informed the doctors, who immediately came to Inouye's aid and tended to his injuries. For 2nd Lt. Daniel Inouye, his days of combat were over.

The western end of the Gothic Line collapsed to the 442nd within mere hours of fighting. By the end of the first day, all units of the 442nd achieved their objectives of taking the enemy strongholds, and the Germans quickly surrendered. With the western end of the Gothic Line now in Allied hands, they were able to fight atop the mountain range toward the eastern shores of Italy.

As they continued moving forward and into the town of Carrara, Kash and his men were pinned down by a machine gun nest in front of an observation post that was held by a battalion of Germans. It was a fierce battle and men were being hit by machine gun fire and artillery. As he was advancing forward, Kash came across an injured 442nd soldier who was exposed to enemy fire. He dragged him to an area where there was an indentation in the ground, applied a tourniquet, and laid him down so he was out of the enemy's line of fire. While Kash didn't want to leave him, the battle continued to rage on and he told the soldier that he would send litter bearers to take him to the aid station when it was safe. The soldier told Kash that he was okay and to go kick ass. Before he could even thank him, Kash was gone.

Kash continued moving cautiously forward toward the machine gun nest that had his men pinned down. He saw that it was so well placed that nobody could move without exposing themselves. Kash realized that the machine gun nest had to be taken out in order for them to continue their advance, and once again took on the incredibly dangerous assignment of taking it out himself instead of ordering any of his men to do it. Gathering his focus and waiting for the perfect time to attack, he suddenly charged and sprinted toward the machine gun nest. As his men saw him attack, they covered his advance by firing their weapons. As Kash attacked firing his Tommy gun, the Germans responded with machine gun fire, spraying bullets all around him, but not a single bullet hit him. His men could not believe what they were seeing. He wiped out the machine gun nest and cleared his men to continue their advance. Sergeant Fred Matsumura would later say that Kash's jacket was riddled with bullet holes from that fight. "Kash had so much guts…I had so much respect for him."

Now that the area was cleared of enemy fire, Kash called upon some of the men to go back and help the injured soldier who needed to be taken to the field hospital.

Kash would later say that "The Germans had a forward observer on the mountaintop, and we couldn't knock it out, so I stood up and charged up the hill to draw fire. You had to expose yourself to see the German's positions, so we took on a company of Germans and we beat them. After that we kept pushing them back and they finally gave up. We ended up with thousands of German prisoners."

For this action, Kash would be awarded a Silver Star, but the Army Chief of Staff's recommendation to award Kash the Distinguished Service Cross for his gallantry under fire was rejected; presumably by Lt. Colonel Pursell.

They continued their forward advance and now had the Germans on the run. Advancing under heavy enemy fire, they came across an area of trees and brush where German soldiers had congregated. Kash ordered his men to prepare their weapons for a bayonet charge. Quietly advancing toward the enemy and getting as close as they could without being detected, Kash gave the order to attack, and they all charged through an open clearing yelling and screaming like mad men, attacking the Germans and again taking them by surprise in hand-to-hand combat, routing the enemy and taking more German prisoners.

As the fighting subsided and the men were securing their positions, the Germans counterattacked. Kash was talking with some of his men near a captured bunker when an artillery shell hit the corner of the bunker and exploded twenty feet from where Kash was standing. A cement block hit Kash in the head and shrapnel ripped through his shoulder. Dazed and stunned, he got up and looked around. His men helped him up and told him that he was bleeding badly and needed to get to the aid station to get patched up. Fortunately, he was not seriously injured and could make it on his own. As he headed to the aid station, he joked with his buddy Beanie about going back "home" to the aid station again. Beanie laughed and Kash gave him his compass and binoculars and told him to take over, and that he would be back soon enough. Kash headed to the aid station and they went their separate ways.

Beanie volunteered to go on patrol with Lt. Sadaichi Kubota, a battlefield-commissioned officer who was Kash's platoon leader, to secure the area and look for German troops who may still be in the area. As Beanie and Lt. Kubota carefully surveyed the area, machine gun fire erupted without warning and they suddenly found themselves in the middle of an ambush, caught in crossfire between two machine gun nests. Lt. Kubota quickly realized they were overwhelmingly outmatched against the German firepower and took cover. As he turned to Beanie and ordered him to return fire, he saw Beanie's lifeless body on the trail where they were attacked. Beanie Hayashi was dead.

Kubota tried desperately to get to Beanie's body but it was no use. Despite never having left a man behind, the Germans had him pinned down. He was forced to make a life and death decision; to try to survive by somehow getting away undetected or recover Beanie's body with a high likelihood of being killed himself. It was a gut-wrenching decision, but the Germans' firepower was overwhelming. Somehow, Lt. Kubota escaped the German crossfire and made his way back to his platoon.

Kash was at the aid station when he heard that Beanie had gone missing. He once again took off before anyone could stop him to find his friend. He met up with Sgt. Fred Matsumura and they both went toward the direction where Beanie had gone on patrol, and were intercepted by Lt. Kubota, who told them about the ambush and Beanie being hit, and the heavy enemy fire that prevented Kubota from pulling Beanie out of there. As Kash started to take off to find Beanie, Kubota ordered him to stand down from searching for him until the area could be secured. Kash was incensed; not only did his platoon leader leave a man behind, but that man was his best friend.

After the hostilities subsided, Lt. Kubota, Kash, and his men went to the area of the ambush and found Beanie's body where he fell. Losing Beanie hit Kash hard. Beanie was his best friend and the only man his squad ever left behind. Kash felt that Beanie would still be alive had he not ordered him to take over, and that Kash would have taken that bullet instead. The guilt was almost overwhelming. Tadao "Beanie" Hayashi's death would haunt both Kash and Lt. Kubota for the rest of their lives. He was the only soldier in Kash's 1st squad to die in World War II.

The Allies moved eastward, routing the German army across the Apennine Mountain range, and on May 2, 1945, twenty-eight days after their monumental victory breaching the Gothic Line, the Germans in Italy surrendered, ending the war in Italy. The Battle of the Gothic Line was an epic victory for the Allies. What the entire American 5th Army could not accomplish over six months in securing the western end of the Gothic Line, the 442nd Regimental Combat Team accomplished in less than forty-eight hours.

Kash at Beanie's gravesite. Courtesy of the Kashino Family.

Italy's surrender on May 2, 1945, was followed by Germany's surrender six days later on May 8, 1945 (Victory in Europe Day). The war in Europe was over, and the 442nd Regimental Combat Team distinguished itself as the most decorated war unit in the history of the United States Army for its size and duration, and Kash was one of the most decorated soldiers in the 442nd. The celebration of the war's end in Europe rang far and wide. Germany surrendered unconditionally and Adolph Hitler was dead. Europe was finally at peace again, and the men of the 442nd not only accomplished their goal of proving their loyalty as Americans to the United States of America, but they also proved their gallantry as American heroes, having been victorious in some of the most epic battles in U.S. history.

Inexplicably, on May 10, 1945, two days after Germany's surrender, Staff Sergeant Shiro "Kash" Kashino, Staff Sergeant Fred Matsumura, and Private First Class James Matsuda, the men who were sent to the stockade for the bar fight in France and later released by Lt. Colonel Pursell to lead their men to victory in the Battle of the Gothic Line, were summoned to trial for the bar fight by none other than Lt. Colonel Pursell himself. All the men thought the charges had been dropped when Pursell released them from the stockade to fight in the battle of the Gothic Line, but now Pursell was bringing them back to face court-martial.

Adding insult to injury, Beanie Hayashi had been killed in action at the Gothic Line. Despite their gallantry in leading their men to victory and helping to achieve what no other army had ever accomplished, it was apparent that nothing but death itself could keep Lt. Colonel Pursell from exacting his revenge on Kash and his men for his insubordination during the Battle of the Lost Battalion. None of the men could believe what was happening.

They brought each man into the court one at a time. Oddly, they were given no legal representation, and the Military Police officer involved in the altercation was neither mentioned nor present. Nonetheless, they respectfully pleaded not guilty. Then on May 18, 1945, four officers found Staff Sergeant Shiro "Kash" Kashino, Staff Sergeant Fred Matsumura, and Private First Class James Matsuda guilty. They were sentenced to six months in the stockade without pay, stripped of their ranks, and busted down to buck private, the lowest rank in the United States Army. It was to be the final tragic irony for Kash of World War II; after all he had done in volunteering out of the Minidoka concentration camp to fight for the United States to prove his loyalty and becoming one of the most decorated soldiers of World War II, he realized that *his entire experience with the U.S. Army began with being wrongly incarcerated in a U.S. Army prison (Minidoka), and now was ending* with being punished, stripped of his rank, and wrongly incarcerated again in a U.S. Army prison (stockade).

As Shiro would write in one of his letters to Louise:

> *Now, here's a little bit of possible disappointment. I thought after I went on line again my troubles back in France would be forgotten but, no, they brought it up again. So after this letter I'll be a private, I hope it doesn't make you feel too bad. But I've also got a little punishment to take. If this case was forgotten I think I could have given you a surprise but well, let's forget the 'ifs.' But honey, one thing, even though I'm not much of a garrison soldier, the boys really respect me for what I am. I've backed them up, took their blames for over a year now, and so in a way don't be ashamed. Well, honey, enuf said for today, and I still love you, and that's plenty of love, miss you, well, just wait till I get back.*
>
> *Love, Shiro*

In September 1945, Kash finished his tour of duty in Switzerland and Germany and boarded a ship back to the States. All his men had already returned to America in July on a 442nd transport while he served out his jail sentence. It was a long ride across the Atlantic Ocean, but this time there were no concerns of German U-boats or any danger of being blown out of the water. The world was finally at peace, and he passed the time making new friends on the ship and looking forward to reuniting with Louise and building a wonderful life with her. So much had happened since the last time he saw her in Chicago before being shipped off to Europe. "Is she excited to see me? Will she love me for the man I am now?" he wondered.

As excited as he was to see her again, he couldn't help but be fearful that her feelings for him might have changed. Despite Kash's reputation as something of a happy-go-lucky flirt, he remained true to Louise throughout all of World War II.

Kash now had to figure out what his next step was going to be. Having accomplished his goals of proving his loyalty to America and surviving the war, it was now time for him to deliver on his promise to Louise of giving her a good life. While Minidoka had not yet closed, it was clear that the government was releasing internees to start anew away from the West Coast, so restarting their lives together in Chicago seemed like a good idea. While he hoped that they could return to Seattle someday, the truth of the matter was that Kash welcomed the idea of living someplace new, away from the discrimination they experienced in the northwest. With no knowledge of the kinds of opportunities that lie ahead for him, Kash resolved to make a go of it in Chicago and do whatever it took to give Louise the good life he promised her.

Louise had continued her studies in business school to become a legal secretary and learned to become independent in her new life in Chicago. Although she was all of nineteen years old at this point, like many Japanese Americans in the days of World War II, she had experienced more of life and tragedy than many people experience in a lifetime. She started her new life in Chicago with only the kindness of the Quaker family who had sponsored her out of Minidoka as she settled into her new surroundings. It was nice for Louise to make some new acquaintances who did not share the kind of bias and prejudice toward Japanese Americans like many on the West Coast. But being so far from her family and friends still left her terribly lonely.

Louise was always thankful for the dozens of Kash's comrades who made a special detour to Chicago to visit her as they headed home from the war. They would tell Louise that they felt as if they already knew her since Kash talked about her so much. She heard story after story about his bravery and how he always took better care of his men than he did of himself, and as always, he never backed down from a fight. It was clear that Kash was admired and respected by those who knew him.

Fred Matsumura would tell her that if not for the unjustified court-martial, Kash would have been at least a Lieutenant, and should have received the Distinguished Service Cross (many of which were later upgraded to the Congressional Medal of Honor). He and others would tell her that Kash was one of a kind, never got mad at his men, and always talked about Louise and what she was doing. Kash was a born leader, gutsy, and an all-around terrific guy. He always went all out to take care of folks. Their stories only made Louise love him that much more and sustained her through her loneliness in Chicago. Through it all, she remained true to Kash and constantly hoped and prayed for his safe return so they could spend the rest of their lives together, and now he was finally coming home to her.

When he got back on U.S. soil in October, and as soon as he was honorably discharged from the Army, Kash headed straight to Chicago for his reunion with Louise. She was at the bus station to greet him. As she waited for his bus to arrive, she recalled the last time she had seen Kash in Chicago, and how desperately sad she was when they said goodbye to each other, knowing that he might be killed and never come back to her. Every day was a day of worry and fear of getting bad news, and every night brought relief of another day passing with no bad news. He was finally coming home to her as he had left; healthy, strong, and in one piece.

When Kash's bus finally arrived, Louise called out to him and they embraced for several minutes, just holding each other. It was the reunion they both feared might never happen and a moment they would remember forever. The worst of their World War II experiences were behind them, and now they could focus on their future together. Despite the trouble Kash had with the Army and Lt. Colonel Pursell, he was happy and grateful to have survived World War II alive and healthy, and never forgot those who lost their lives or were permanently scarred by the war. He resolved to live his life with gratitude that he came home alive and focus on fulfilling his promise to Louise of building a good life for her.

10

Heroes Not Welcome

The ten internment camps were gradually evacuated and shuttered, with the last of them closing in March 1946. Minidoka closed in October 1945, with every internee given a one-way bus ticket and $25 to start a new life or pick up where they left off. While most of the folks were elated to be released from the most terrible experience of their lives, many were distraught and devastated at being uprooted yet again. Despite how terrible it was living in Minidoka, the Japanese inmates had made it their home for three years, building communities and cultivating the land. It was the Japanese inmates of Minidoka who brought irrigation to the Idaho desert, and it had become a community that many didn't want to leave, but they were given no choice.

What made it most difficult was that first they were forced from their homes and placed into the Minidoka concentration camp, and now many were being evicted from Minidoka and left effectively homeless. Many families lost everything because of Executive Order 9066. Farms, businesses, personal property, and homes were extorted for pennies on the dollar, never to be returned to their rightful owners. Worse, many folks who had trusted friends and acquaintances to take care of their belongings found everything to have been lost or stolen when they returned from the internment camps. What should have been a happy homecoming turned out to be a terrible disappointment for many, with yet another treasured part of their lives taken away.

Mr. and Mrs. Tsuboi stayed in Minidoka until it closed in October 1945. At first, they were excited to get back to their belongings they left in their neighbor's boarding house in Seattle and restart their lives. But as they were finalizing their plans for their return to Seattle, they learned the heartbreaking news that their neighbor with whom they entrusted their belongings had disappeared. Everything was gone. It was a level of betrayal that they never expected. Brokenhearted, the Tsubois and many other families decided that they could not stomach returning to Seattle where so many terrible memories haunted them, so they decided instead to start a new life in Minneapolis.

Kash and Louise married on December 1, 1945. Mrs. Tsuboi made arrangements for their wedding in Minneapolis and made food (including Kash's favorite sushi) and refreshments for the minister, his wife, and a small group of guests. It was a day that was a long time coming. Two days later, Kash and Louise returned to Chicago, and instead of spending their honeymoon in New York City, they opted to buy furniture for their new apartment, which they felt truly fortunate to get.

They stayed in Chicago through 1946, during which time Kash went to Chicago Technical College to be an air conditioning and HVAC repairman while Louise continued her studies. Unfortunately, he could not find work since the unions in Chicago would not accept Japanese Americans as members. Despite the war having ended with the Japanese surrender on September 2, 1945, and with Kash and the men of the 442nd

Louise and Shiro Kashino's wedding picture in December, 1945.
Photo courtesy of the Kashino Family

being among the most decorated American heroes in all of World War II, discrimination and prejudice continued to plague Japanese Americans well after the war. So, with the war over, all the internment camps closed, and the internees free to resume and rebuild their lives, Kash and Louise packed their bags and moved back home to Seattle.

Upon returning to Seattle, Kash continued to have a tough time finding a job. He tried to get into the pipefitters union but was told that he would not be accepted because the jobs were being saved for returning American veterans. Although he explained that he was an American World War II veteran, they still kept him out. And the air conditioning classes he took in Chicago were never put to use, because he found those jobs closed to Japanese Americans as well.

Finally, he was offered a job back at Tashiro Hardware, which had reopened after the war. The owner welcomed him back with open arms, and it was exactly the opportunity he and Louise needed to get them on their feet. While it didn't pay much, it was enough for them to rent a small apartment and begin their new life back in Seattle. Kash didn't give up his efforts to build a better life for Louise, and eventually landed a successful career as a car salesman, a job that he loved and kept until his retirement, while Louise also settled into her career as a legal secretary at a restaurant supply company.

Like Louise's family, many families returned to Seattle only to find that the people who promised to care for their homes, businesses, and belongings had betrayed them, and they were relegated to starting all over again. Kash and Louise spent much of their time helping other Japanese American families get resettled and rebuild the Japanese American community in Seattle. Kash had left Seattle with nothing but the clothes on his back, so for him, returning to Seattle meant a new start with the added pride of knowing that he had proved his loyalty—as did many of his comrades of Japanese ancestry—to the United States of America. But some things did not change.

Having gone through the hell of war, and experiencing the physical and mental agony of battle, Kash came back to Seattle a hardened combat veteran. And although he was a highly decorated hero of the United States Army, Kash and Louise continued to feel treated as though they were at fault for the war with Japan. Although most people at least tolerated, and even welcomed, the returning former inmates of the internment camps, pockets of racism and prejudice against people of Japanese ancestry remained. Many faced continued discrimination as they sought to restart their lives back home on the West Coast.

When Minidoka internees returned to Seattle, some came home to threatening graffiti and vandalized property. Despite Japanese Americans proving their loyalty during World War II, racism against Japanese Americans continued. Photo courtesy of the Museum of History and Industry.

Louise would later say that even after they returned to Seattle, Kash continued to set the record straight against anyone who called him a Jap. "Boy, if anyone called him that, ka-pow!"

Kash would later recall a day when there was a big fight at a boathouse on Harbor Island. "This guy and his buddies called me and my friends 'dirty Japs' and took us outside, so we took them on and beat the daylights out of 'em. They respected us after that. Same thing happened in Chinatown. We had lotsa fights because of derogatory remarks, but we knew how to fight so we always won."

Kash's friends would later recall that whenever Kash would say "Here, hold my glasses," someone was about to get clobbered. Kash never did, and never would accept anyone calling him a "Jap," let alone a dirty one. As time went on, the derogatory remarks became less frequent and Kash became more constrained in his interactions with bigots.

In the previous year, while Kash and Louise were in Chicago, veterans of the 442nd in Seattle applied to join the Veterans of Foreign Wars (VFW). But despite the heroics and recognition by the United States Army of the 442nd, the American veterans were denied membership to the VFW because of their Japanese ancestry. They were stunned to find such prejudice in the VFW of all places, even after having proven their loyalty and valor in the United States Army.

Undaunted, the 442nd veterans started a Japanese American veteran's group called the Nisei Veteran's Committee (NVC). As they searched for a building for their new organization, the Seattle Kendo Club stepped up and sold a large building to the NVC for $1,000 in honor of the heroism of the men of the 442nd. All they asked was for the building to be used to support the Japanese American community, and the men of the NVC wholeheartedly agreed.

After returning to Seattle in 1947, Kash became the second Commander of the NVC, during which time he led an effort to erect a monument for those Japanese Americans killed in the line of duty. This was to be a tremendous challenge, especially since the cost of what Kash had envisioned would be over $10,000 (over $100,000 in 2023 dollars), so the call went out for donations, and they raised the money they needed. In 1956, the Nisei War Memorial was dedicated at Lake View Cemetery in Seattle, Washington, where it stands to this day to honor Japanese Americans from the northwest who made the ultimate sacrifice in service to the United States of America.

Kash and Louise had their first child in 1949, a baby girl named Kristine Ann. With a growing family, Kash and Louise decided to buy a house. But buying a house as Japanese Americans was not so easy. When Louise and Kash visited the office of a realtor to inquire about buying a house in West Seattle, the realtor told them that a certain area was for American veterans, at which time Kash explained that he was an American veteran. When the realtor continued to refuse, Kash stood up and chased the realtor around his desk and out of his office. They were finally able to purchase their first home in the Madrona neighborhood in Seattle, and in 1950 the couple had their second child, Debbra Lee. Suddenly, Kash found himself with two beautiful daughters, the bright futures and freedom for whom Kash had fought so valiantly for in World War II. He had always lived by the motto of his Hawaiian comrades, "Kodomo no tame ni," which meant "For the sake of the children" in Japanese, and now he could relish in knowing that he made a difference in his children's future.

In 1953, Kash was notified that the first reunion for the Nisei veterans of the 100th/442nd/Military Intelligence Service (MIS) was to be hosted in Hawaii. Although Kash desperately wanted to see his comrades in arms again to rekindle friendships, talk story, and remember friends lost in World War II, there was no way he would be able to afford such a tremendously expensive trip. As it turned out, a bunch of guys in the 442nd desperately wanted Kash to join them too, so they started a collection and gave Kash an

Kash is welcomed to Hawaii with leis from men and families of the 442nd, many of whom pitched in to pay for Kash's trip to Hawaii for the first reunion of the 442nd Regimental Combat Team. Photo courtesy of the Kashino family.

all-expense-paid trip to Hawaii so he could participate in the first reunion of the 442nd.

The Kashino family continued to grow in 1956, with the birth of Beverly Sue, and they again decided to find a larger home. As they looked at a new development of homes in Rainier Beach, the realtor signaled that they were out of bounds of where Japanese Americans would be accepted. This was eleven years after World War II had ended. They were not even shown homes east of 50th (near the lake), and in Kash's words, "There was still lots of discrimination, especially in real estate." But they eventually found a home in South Seattle above Seward Park, which would be their home for forty years.

The reunion of the 100th/442nd/MIS of 1961 was the first time Kash attended the reunion with his family. They scrimped and saved for the entire year, and Debbie Kashino recalled that her parents would buy the girls one pair of shoes every September that had to last the whole school year. When they went to Hawaii in June, they were allowed to buy party shoes for the trip, which made their journey especially memorable for her. For Louise and the girls, the reunion was an incredible experience. When they arrived in Honolulu at 2:00 a.m., dozens of people were there to meet them. This was the first time the Kashino family had experienced the love that the men of the 442nd had for their dad, who was a hero to many heroes of the 442nd.

This photo, taken in 1961 is of Kash, Louise, and their three daughters, Debbra, Beverly, and Kris... and their party shoes as they arrived in Hawaii. Photo courtesy of the Kashino family.

For Louise, it was an opportunity to see the men she had met as they journeyed home from the war. It was also her first time to hear about some of Kash's experiences since he never talked about his war experiences at home. But once he was with his buddies, she was able to hear stories about how brave and caring—and crazy—Kash had been in battle. It was an emotional rollercoaster the entire time, one minute laughing uncontrollably about memories, and the next minute reminiscing on battle experiences and lost friends. It was an experience Louise would never forget, and she knew that these were unbreakable bonds that would last for the rest of Kash's life.

Pearl Harbor Day Surprise

It happened during dinner on Monday, December 8, 1969. Kash came home from work and Louise had dinner on the table when Beverly explained that during American history class, the teacher discussed Pearl Harbor Day. All of her classmates turned around and gave Beverly dirty looks, as though she was the enemy. She went on to say she hated Pearl Harbor because of the other students' reactions and asked her dad, "What side were you on, the American or Japanese side?"

Louise gently told Beverly to advise the other students that her dad was an American war hero, one of the most decorated American heroes of all time. Upon learning that her dad was a hero not for the Japanese Army, but for the United States Army, Beverly was suddenly relieved and proud at the same time; her dad not only fought in the United States Army, but he was also an American hero.

Although they had attended several 442nd reunions, Louise and Kash were shocked that through it all, Bev thought her dad's gallantry had been for the *Japanese* Army. It made them realize that they had not spoken enough about their World War II experiences. Kash would later say, "(Our children) knew I fought in the Army, but it turns out they didn't know which Army!"

Being a humble man who never talked about himself, Kash kept all his medals stashed away in a Crown Royal bag he kept in his dresser drawer. While Kash and his fellow veterans would relive battles, debate strategies, and share stories of lost comrades at their reunions and the NVC, looking back, he realized that where their families were concerned, they never spelled it out that much. "We presumed they knew, but maybe they didn't. War is hell. We thought that the less they knew the better."

Kash and Louise would go on to raise a wonderful family and be happily married for fifty-two years. And through it all, Louise was the one who often "wore the pants" in the family. She raised the girls to be strong and independent, and always willing to help others. Louise was smart, meticulous, and felt strongly about putting effort into always looking your best. As their daughters would later say, "Behind every great man is a great woman."

Since Kash was color blind, Louise always helped him to match his clothes, so he was always impeccably dressed as a sales manager for Bill Pierre Ford in Seattle. And they *always* had cool cars. He was also a creature of habit, going through the same routine day after day of waking up at a certain time, polishing his shoes, eating breakfast, going through his bathroom routine, going to work, and then coming home for dinner with the family at the same time every day. And when it came to their daughters, Kash was scary to boys who wanted to date them; especially the boys he didn't like. Their vacations became routine as well, spending their summer vacations every year in Lake Chelan. It was to become a tradition that would last for over sixty years.

Kash always taught his kids to take pride in working hard and doing their best and was very responsible with his money. While he was a big spender, he was a "cash and carry" man who only bought what he could pay for in cash. He was also a great saver, as he stuffed money in all kinds of places: books, hats, pillows, and especially his golf bag. His family learned to never throw anything away without checking it twice for hidden treasures. They also always had a dog; mostly males since he was outnumbered by females in his household.

In addition to supporting his family, Kash spent much of his life supporting the Japanese American community, often at times when nobody knew he was doing it. In the early 1970s, some of the third-generation Japanese kids (Sanseis) were seriously into drugs. Over thirty-five teenagers became addicted to heroin and were enrolled in a methadone clinic in Seattle. On occasion, some of the kids would get into trouble with the police, who would call Kash to take care of them. Kash had been deputized by the Seattle Police Department, so when the youngsters got caught, the police transferred them into his care. In cases where the kids overdosed after the clinic closed for the day, Kash would call a close friend of his, Dr. Ben Uyeno, one of six physicians who could prescribe methadone, a drug used to tide addicts over for a day as they tried to stop their addiction. Kash and Dr. Uyeno would lecture the boys, but also knew it was up to the youngsters to get help and work through it. After giving them the proper dosage of methadone, Kash made sure they got home safely. Dr. Uyeno would later say that in the spirit of not wanting the parents to suffer, Kash never told anyone, and he was certain that most of the parents never knew the extent to which he helped their kids.

Kash's family was completely unaware of what he and Dr Uyeno did to help the teens until 2001, when Dr. Uyeno wrote Louise a letter of confidential recognition for Kash's civilian heroism and concern for those who lived in the community. Kash knew all the Sansei but had kept his interactions with them strictly confidential for all those years. It was classic Kash; always helping others and never talking about it or expecting anything in return. In Dr. Uyeno's words, "Kash was amazing that way."

Tragedy struck in 1984, when Tadao "Beanie" Hayashi's brother—the same Beanie Hayashi who was killed in action at the Gothic

Line—visited Kash and Louise in Seattle with his wife. Kash was driving a van from the car dealership and was making a left turn under Highway 99 in Seattle, when an oncoming car driving 100 miles per hour crashed into the passenger side of the van. The car was driving so fast that it caught Kash completely unaware. The impact caused some of the passengers to be ejected out of the van, landing on and around the railroad tracks. Tragically, Beanie's brother died in the accident, and his wife was seriously injured. Louise had been driving in another car following the van and saw everything that happened.

Kash was heartbroken, and his crushing loss was only exacerbated by having to serve as a witness at the trial of the other driver for vehicular homicide, where Kash had to repeatedly relive the accident and that terrible moment. He had a perfect driving record with no accidents up to that point, which was now shattered by his best friend's brother having been killed. Kash was devastated. He had lived through World War II having done everything he could to keep his men as safe as possible, and Beanie was the only man in his squad who died after taking a bullet that Kash believed was meant for himself. And now, nearly forty years later, Kash blamed himself for not protecting Beanie's brother from dying in Seattle. It launched Kash into a level of distress and depression he would never recover from, and many close to him would later say contributed to his cancer five years later.

When he was diagnosed with cancer in 1989, Kash decided to use the remaining time in his life to share his experiences from World War II. He was always reluctant to talk about his experiences during the war, but after learning of his cancer, Kash started talking more about his war experiences on TV, radio, and in various interviews. He was very proud of having opened the doors of freedom for future generations of Japanese Americans, and felt strongly that much of the progress that happened after the war was greatly influenced by the 442nd having fought for the United States so valiantly in World War II. Now he wanted to spend the rest of his life doing his part to keep the memory alive of the history of the Japanese American concentration camps, and especially that of the Japanese American soldiers of the 442nd who had fought so bravely and made such terrific sacrifices to be recognized as loyal and patriotic Americans.

Despite having been busted down from Staff Sergeant to the lowest rank in the U.S. military and having lived with the disgrace of an unjustified court-martial conviction until the day he died, Kash lived with a level of honor and gratitude that only those who knew him could understand. He never begrudged the United States Army or government. To the contrary, he was grateful for having lived through World War II and the chance to provide a life of freedom and opportunity for Louise, their family, and future generations of Japanese Americans.

Kash was proud and grateful that the courage and sacrifices made by the men of the 442nd RCT contributed to America recognizing Japanese Americans as loyal and patriotic citizens of the United States.

Kash and Louise in 1994. They were true American heroes. Photo courtesy of the Kashino family

11

His Final Battle

It happened at the 442nd reunion in 1983. Some of the men were teasing Kash, calling him the "SNAFU Guy" because of his court-martial and having been demoted to private. Although everyone knew about Kash's heroics, they also knew the story of his court-martial and some would not let him forget it, even though it was something that had happened nearly forty years in the past. Kash always brushed it off and took it all in stride. It was all in the past and he knew in his heart that he always did what he thought was right and had served with honor.

Listening in on the joking was Lieutenant Sadaichi Kubota, who was Kash's platoon leader during the war. He was intimately aware of what had happened and the unfairness of Kash's court-martial. While Kash laughed it all off, Kubota took considerable offense to the teasing, especially since Kash was convicted for a crime he didn't commit. It was at that moment that Kubota resolved to clear Kash's name and get his rank restored to Staff Sergeant, despite knowing that it wasn't going to be easy, especially since nearly four decades had passed.

The first challenge was to convince Kash to re-enter the world of the United States Army once again on a low-odds mission to clear his name. Kash had long since put that episode in his life behind him and had no intention of reliving it all over only to be embarrassed and disappointed again. He considered it water under the bridge that evaporated a long time ago, and just wanted to keep moving forward, grateful to be alive. Despite Kubota's encouragement to at least give it a shot and see what happened, Kash had made up his mind that what was done was done, and to let sleeping dogs lie.

Refusing to give up, Kubota reached out to Louise for her help in convincing Kash to clear his name. Since Kash had never shared any details of the situation that resulted in his court-martial forty years prior, Kubota told her the entire story about how he was arrested, court-martialed, and demoted for a crime he didn't commit. As she knew Kash as the intensely humble and proud man that he was, she wasn't surprised that he never talked about his conviction and demotion, however unjust it might have been. Now that she understood what happened and that Kubota was willing to right a wrong, albeit one committed so long ago, she decided to encourage her husband to work with Kubota to clear his name and have his rank restored to Staff Sergeant for his daughters. If he was wrongfully convicted, she wanted it to be corrected in the name of justice. Finally, in 1985, after two years of encouragement and coaxing, Kash agreed to move forward to clear his name and get his rank restored to Staff Sergeant despite having no guarantees that they would be successful, again for the sake of the children.

Fred Matsumura, who was also court-martialed and demoted with Kash for the bar incident in France, had also refused to pursue efforts to clear his name. But he, too, eventually acquiesced and agreed to join the effort to overturn his and Kash's convictions. With Kash's and Fred's approvals finally secured, they launched their plan of attack with a visit to Washington, DC. There they met with U.S. House Representative Patsy Mink and U.S. Senators Daniel Inouye and Spark Matsunaga, both of whom had served in the 100th Battalion and the 442nd RCT. All three enthusiastically agreed to support their efforts and shared their understanding of how the process typically worked and who they needed to contact, with the first being the United States Army Personnel Records Center to get copies of Kash's Army and court-martial records.

It was with bitter disappointment that they learned that Kash's Army records had been destroyed in a fire at the Personnel Records Center in 1973. Without Kash's and Fred's records, it was impossible to move forward. After two years of encouragement and getting their hopes up, Kash and Fred could not believe that all was lost so quickly. It was over and their quest came to an end with an immediate and unceremonious thud.

In the following weeks, Kubota shared Kash's situation and their bitter disappointment with another 442nd veteran, Bill Thompson. Although Thompson had not fought with Kash, he knew who he was and offered to assist in their efforts. For years, Kubota and Thompson looked for different paths forward despite Kash's records having been destroyed, but every path led to a dead end. It seemed that all was lost, until finally in 1995, ten years after they learned Kash's records were destroyed, a breakthrough came when his records were miraculously located. The copies mailed to them were singed and showed evidence of having been in a fire, but his records were thankfully intact and entirely legible. Suddenly, a breath of new life was given to the quest.

When Kash received the call from Kubota informing him of the good news that his Army records had been found, he didn't know if he should be pleased with the news or weary of restarting a low-odds effort that, in his mind, would likely end in disappointment as it had ten years prior. Louise's reaction to the news was of instant excitement, and it didn't take long for her to convince Kash that it was an opportunity not to be dismissed. So, with a renewed hope, Kash, Louise, Sadaichi Kubota, and Bill Thompson got busy and went to work.

Using Kash's Army records to build their case to get his conviction overturned and his rank reinstated, Kubota and Thompson tracked down James Matsuda, the 442nd soldier who punched the Military Police officer in 1945. After meeting with him twice, they finally convinced him to admit that he was the one who caused the scuffle with the MP resulting in three innocent men being thrown into the stockade. Although reluctant, he admitted that his refusal to accept and admit responsibility for the incident had haunted him for all those years. To Kubota's and Thompson's great relief and appreciation, Matsuda submitted a signed affidavit admitting his guilt and exonerating Kash, Fred Matsumura, and Beanie Hayashi, who died during the battle of the Gothic Line.

With renewed hope and tremendous anticipation, they continued to build and document their case, and submitted the application to the Army Board for Correction of Military Records requesting that Kash's rank of staff sergeant be reinstated and included Matsuda's affidavit proving Kash's innocence. After having been turned down twice, the group decided to submit his application one last time. To everyone's jubilation, the third time proved to be a charm and a favorable decision was granted restoring Kash's rank and giving him back pay for the six months he spent in the stockade. Kash was elated. Finally, after all those years, he was once again recognized by the United States Army as a staff sergeant. Most importantly to Kash, his grave marker would show him having been a staff sergeant and not a private. It was a moment of celebration for Kash as he would forever be remembered and honored as Staff Sergeant Shiro "Kash" Kashino.

While getting his rank reinstated was indeed cause for celebration, the next and final step would prove to be even more daunting, since getting his court-martial conviction overturned was an entirely different matter. Although Kash's health was becoming more fragile from battling cancer, he and Louise were excited to continue the momentum of their victory in restoring his rank and resolved to take the fight of having his court-martial dismissed to the bitter end.

The biggest hurdle they had to overcome was that the statute of limitations to appeal Kash's Article 69 special court-martial had expired in 1983, and the only person who could overturn his conviction was the United States Judge Advocate General himself (JAG), who would only consider their case if new evidence was presented that was unattainable within the original statute of limitations. Now all they had to do was to figure it out.

As they filed through Kash's recovered records, they found that the court-martial order said that private Shiro Kashino pleaded guilty to the charges of 1. Resisting the MPs by trying to take Tadao Hayashi away, and 2. Drunk and disrespectful conduct toward a superior officer. The records also indicated that Kash had received a copy of the court-martial—which he never did—and he certainly did not plead guilty. The documents showed that the officers who attended the proceedings included Lt. Jorge Suro, the MP officer who was struck by Matsuda during the tavern brawl, but Lt. Suro did not in fact attend the court-martial and Kash knew that he never pressed charges. Now the fate of overturning Kash's court-martial depended on finding Lt. Jorge Suro, Jr. and getting a signed affidavit from him stating that he never pressed charges and had wanted the charges dropped. It might be the new evidence required by the JAG to consider Kash's appeal beyond the original statute of limitations but finding Lt. Suro after five decades would be like finding a needle in a haystack, and they had no way of knowing if he was even alive.

As fate would have it, Clarence Taba, who was Kash's 1st Sergeant during the war and the director of the Hawaii Bank Association at the time, was attending a bankers' conference in Waikiki when he struck up a conversation with a banker from Puerto Rico, Arturo Carrion. He shared Kash's story and told Mr. Carrion that they were looking for a Puerto Rican MP Officer from World War II named Lt. Jorge Suro. To Clarence's astonishment, Mr. Carrion said that Jorge Suro was a good friend of his and a colonel in the Puerto Rico National Guard, and that he would be delighted to connect them. Several months later, after recovering from health issues, Col. Jorge Suro signed an affidavit saying that he never pressed charges against Kash, Fred Matsumura, or James Matsuda and he wanted the charges dropped. The following is the complete text of the affidavit, notarized by Victor R. Gonzales Mangual, esq. on June 4, 1997:

TO WHOM IT MAY CONCERN:

In November 1996, I was contacted by a World War II veteran of the 442nd Regimental Combat Team. Arrangements for this meeting were made by a mutual friend who had visited Hawaii for a banker's conference. Information on an incident which occurred during World War II, while I was stationed in Southern France, was being sought.

The incident referred to occurred on or about February 14, 1945, at a bar in Southern France in the vicinity of Menton. I was a 1st Lieutenant in the 65th Infantry Regiment from Puerto Rico. At that time, I was assigned to the 44th AAA Brigade as an MP officer. On that date, I was making my rounds with a French officer (of the Maquis) when I stopped to question a soldier in a barroom. Without warning, he suddenly turned upon me. It became a scuffle and soon other soldiers were involved. There were soldiers shouting and shoving to stop the fray. Things happened fast but I recall that order was restored after a few minutes or so.

Since it is over fifty years ago that this incident occurred, I do not recall the exact details; however, I do recall that the soldiers, who were from the 442nd Regimental Combat Team, expressed regrets over the incident and went back to their quarters. No arrests were made, no names were taken down—we shook hands over what seemed to have been a misunderstanding. I filed a report on this incident; I do not recall lodging formal charges.

A short while later I discovered that charges were being made against some of the men. I distinctly recall speaking over the phone to the detachment (or unit) commander who had a chaplain on the line during our conversation. Their names have been forgotten. I specifically requested that the charges be dropped. I did not feel a court-martial was warranted. I do not recall the particulars of our conversation nor what transpired subsequently.

In mid-March of 1945, the 442nd Regimental Combat Team prepared for movement to another theater of operation, Italy. As no court-martial trial was held, I assumed the charges against the soldiers involved in the barroom scuffle had been dropped.

Imagine my surprise to learn in November 1996, after over fifty years, that the soldiers had been court-martialed. I would like to state that I was not aware of the Special Court-Martial of S/Sgt. Shiro Kashino and the others until I was provided a copy of the Special Court-Martial Orders No. 18 dated May 20, 1945. I had no knowledge of the trial, much less requested to appear. In closing, I would like to affirm that, as stated above, I did request that charges against the soldiers involved in the incident which occurred on or about February 14, 1945, be dropped.

Dated this 31st day of May, 1997.
(signed) Jorge Suro, Jr., Colonel, Ret.
Affidavit No. 3331

On June 11, 1997, as soon as Bill Thompson received Col. Suro's affidavit, he called Louise to tell her the wonderful news. Sadly, Louise told Bill that Kash had just passed away earlier that same day after his six-year battle with cancer. While she was delighted to see the affidavit of their star witness, Louise was devastated that Kash died before receiving it and with the final judgment of overturning his court-martial still outstanding.

At his bedside before he died, Louise promised her beloved husband that she would fight to the end to get his name cleared. Two days later, in the midst of her grief but with high hopes, Louise, who had courageously stood by Kash throughout those trying months, submitted her appeal to the Judge Advocate General on June 13, 1997. Included in her application were the affidavits of James Matsuda saying that it was he who punched the MP officer so many years prior, and that of Colonel Jorge Suro, Jr. saying that he never pressed charges and wanted the charges dropped. Louise presented the affidavits as information that was unattainable during the original statute of limitations, and as such should be considered as the justification to have Kash's court-martial overturned. All that was left to do at that point was to wait for the JAG's response.

Several weeks later, Louise was disappointed to receive a response from the JAG declining her request to reverse Kash's court-martial. Disappointed but undeterred, Louise, Kubota, and Bill Thompson were not about to give up. They had come too far and worked too hard to give up so easily, so they once again asked Senator Daniel Inouye for his help. His office connected them with a colonel in the JAG's office, who said that the first rejection was likely a standard form letter and encouraged Louise to continue their appeal. They knew from Rep. Patsy Mink that getting the JAG to overturn a conviction was hard, and the only other alternative was a pardon by the President of the United States himself, which was all but impossible. So once again, with renewed hope of a positive outcome, Louise sent a final letter directly to Major General Walter B. Huffman, the Judge Advocate General of the Department of the Army, on October 7, 1997, with a personal and heartfelt plea requesting his consideration in overturning Kash's conviction. Everyone knew it was their last and final hope:

Dear Sir:

SUBJECT: Application for Relief of Shiro Kashino, ASSN: 349-24-6322

By your letter dated September 17, 1997, I was notified that the application of my deceased husband, Shiro Kashino, was denied by your office. My husband knew he was facing a formidable task in 1985 when he embarked on his quest to correct what he deemed to be a wrongful Special Court-Martial Trial. It took him ten years to retrieve his Special Court-Martial orders. Only then could he start to clear his war record. This would not have been possible without the help of his wartime comrades. I am disappointed that relief was not granted and thought of dropping this matter as I have no experience with the military or its policies. But, at his insistence and with the assistance of his wartime comrades, I feel compelled to pursue this matter. I earnestly beseech your office to reconsider the decision to deny his application.

When the Army Board for Correction of Military Records received my husband's applications for correction of records, he was turned down—twice. The Army Board felt that while he presented a forceful case, he did lack certain vital evidence. They suggested specific items he needed in order to validate his claim. With the untiring efforts of his buddies, he did find the evidence which the Army Board had referred to. He re-submitted his application with this new evidence: the Army Board decided in his favor this time. His rank was restored, and his fines rescinded in August 1996. It was an emotional moment for him.

My husband's offense was based on an incident at a bar in Southern France as described in his testimony. His unit had been assigned to the Maritime Alps region to rest and re-group following their epic battle in the Vosges Mountains in northeastern France where, as part of the 36th Texas Division, they wrested a key transportation center from the enemy. His unit was also involved in the rescue of a trapped unit of the 36th, the "Lost Battalion."

My husband's application dated May 30, 1997, and his sworn testimony which I submitted under letter dated June 13, 1997, cited several reasons why my husband felt the Special Court-Martial was in error. I felt encouraged when I learned about a month after submitting his application that Col. Brian X. Bush, Chief, Criminal Law Division, had written to the Honorable Patsy T. Mink, U.S. Representative, on July 18, 1997, stating the application would be processed as expeditiously as possible and your office would require ninety days or so to investigate the application. I was elated, feeling that a thorough examination was being carried out. I, as well as his friends, did not realize that the application would be subsequently denied—abruptly without explanatory details.

I would like to add that efforts were made to locate all those who were connected or familiar with the trial. The executive officer of the unit, James M. Hanley, who called my husband while in battle to discuss the charges was contacted. His address is . . . Col. Hanley does not recall anything of the court-martial. He is in his eighties and in poor health.

The name of T.M. Kobayashi, 2nd Lt., Asst. Adjutant, is shown on Special Court-Martial Orders No. 18. He too was contacted but is in very ill health. He claims he does not remember the court-martial trial, nor anyone connected with the trial. We thought he could direct us to at least one of the presiding officers. He stated that he probably signed the orders as a routine matter and not as a trial participant. His last address in March 1997 was . . . Kobayashi, who retired as a Colonel, U.S. Army, mentioned that he was planning to enter an assisted-care facility at . . . for health reasons.

Until his records were recovered in 1995, my husband did not have any written information concerning his trial. After reading Special Court-Martial Order No. 18, it was apparent that what was most important and missing at his trial was the alleged aggrieved officer. Only then did my husband learn the name of the officer involved, 1st Lt. Jorge Suro, Jr. Why was he not at the trial? My husband did not know how to contact him; we only knew he was with the 65th Infantry, a unit from Puerto Rico. Our friends in Hawaii tried several ways to locate him. It was by chance that we met a Puerto Rican banker attending a conference in Hawaii who gave us his address. The banker stated that Jorge Suro, Jr. was his friend. A war-time buddy of my husband had occasion to go to Puerto Rico for business and made arrangements to meet with Jorge Suro, Jr., a retired Colonel of the Puerto Rico National Guard. His address is . . . Imagine our surprise and elation when Col. Suro recalled the incident.

His recollection that he had asked that charges be dropped gave us new and inspired hope. Col. Suro remembered the incident—he verified that those at the bar shook hands after things had calmed down, agreeing that it was a misunderstanding; he remembered requesting the unit commanding officer to drop charges after he learned about it; and he does not recall being asked to testify at the trial as he had no knowledge of what ensued after my husband's unit left France to fight its last battle in Italy. Col. Suro, Jr., submitted a sworn affidavit on the incident and his role; this is Exhibit D in the application. My husband felt this was the "good cause for failure to file within that time." This newly discovered evidence was not known by my husband until this year. As my husband mentioned in his application, he had been re-confined in the stockade after the surrender of the Germans and released just before the Japanese surrendered. The euphoria over the end of the war both in Europe and the Pacific made my husband's plight inconsequential to others in light of the events of that time.

We had hoped that your office would uncover other details of the trial that we could not find. For example, who was the actual accuser at the trial if the alleged aggrieved officer did not press charges? Shouldn't there have been a defense counsel to assist my husband? Why was there an undue delay in convening the trial which worked against my husband?

If the failure to file by October 1, 1983, is a firm and inflexible rule, then we have no choice but to accept your decision. However, we all felt that if good cause was established the statute of limitations could be extended. This was the basis for the application with the new-found evidence. My husband felt that he did not receive a fair trial as critical evidence was not presented; his trial seemed one of questionable judicial and procedural errors. The critical evidence, unknown to my husband until just before he passed away, is the sworn affidavit of Col. Suro, Jr. This is what my husband considered to be his "...good cause for failure to file within that time." If that is deficient, how may we comply? Neither my husband nor his friends have had experience in military trial procedures. We realize over fifty years have passed, but relevant facts to dismiss my husband's conviction have finally been gathered. I sincerely hope your review will lead to this conclusion.

I respectfully request your reconsideration of the decision to deny the Application for Relief of Shiro Kashino, and do so with the best wishes and prayers of my husband's war-time comrades. I am committed to carrying out my husband's "last battle" to clear his Army record—what he considered to be a precious legacy to his family. If his application can be reconsidered and the stigma of a court-martial of dubious circumstances erased, we will all be grateful knowing that justice has been served and my husband vindicated. If the application is once again denied, my only consolation will be the fact that he died not knowing that he had lost his "last battle."

Thank you for allowing me to plead his case.
Respectfully submitted,
Mrs. Louise (Shiro) Kashino

Louise had no idea how long it would take to get a response, if ever. The encouragement she received from all who supported her kept her faith strong. She knew and believed in her heart that what she was doing was right, and that she had done everything she could and uncovered every stone with the help of Sadaichi Kubota, Bill Thompson, and members of the United States Congress. While she could not imagine anything but a positive response from the JAG, the possibility of a denial to overturn her husband's court-martial haunted her through many sleepless nights. Finally, in December of 1997, Louise received a letter from Major General Walter B. Huffman, the Judge Advocate General. With her heart racing, Louise opened and read the letter advising her of his decision:

DEPARTMENT OF THE ARMY
OFFICE OF THE JUDGE ADVOCATE GENERAL
2200 ARMY PENTAGON
WASHINGTON, DC 20310-2200

December 9, 1997

REPLY TO
ATTENTION OF

The Judge Advocate General

Rec'd 12/15

Mrs. Louise Kashino
5020 48th Avenue, S.
Seattle, Washington 98118

Dear Mrs. Kashino:

    This responds to your letter of October 7, 1997, in which you request reconsideration of my action on your husband's application for relief under Article 69(b), Uniform Code of Military Justice. I have carefully considered this matter and the points you raise in your letter.

    Based on the entire file and the information provided in all documents submitted with this appeal, I have determined that there is "good cause" in the interests of justice to consider this appeal even though it was not filed within the statute of limitations. Mr. Kashino's appeal is granted and his court-martial conviction is set aside.

    You have my sincere sympathy for your husband's death. Your husband was deeply concerned over this event in his life, and your letter eloquently details his extraordinary efforts to erase the court-martial conviction from his record. I am particularly impressed by your husband's gallantry and the six Purple Hearts he earned during World War II. I wish you the very best in the future.

Sincerely,

Your husband was an American Hero — and that is how he should be remembered. WBH

Walter B. Huffman
Major General, U.S. Army
The Judge Advocate General

Enclosure

While the Judge Advocate General's letter reversing Kash's court-martial conviction was cause for great celebration, Louise's only regret was that Kash couldn't be with her to share in his final victory. Photo courtesy of the Kashino family

Kash's conviction had been overturned. At the end of his letter, General Huffman hand-wrote: *"Your husband was an American hero —and that is how he should be remembered."*

It was wonderful news for the Kashino family. Kash was vindicated, but their hard-fought battle was also bittersweet with Kash having passed away five months earlier. The hardest thing for Louise was that Kash wasn't with her when she received General Huffman's letter, but they were comforted in Staff Sergeant Shiro "Kash" Kashino's final victory and vindication over an injustice that he had lived with until the day he died. He never lost a battle during World War II, and his perfect lifetime battle record against racism, discrimination, injustice, and enemies of America was now complete.

12

Valor Undefeated

Shiro "Kash" Kashino was honorably discharged from the United States Army in September 1945. For his courageous service in the United States Army, amassing one of the most decorated war records in World War II, the official military records of Shiro Kashino, 39 919 567, show entitlement to the following decorations and awards:

- Silver Star
- Bronze Star Medal for Heroism with "V" Device
- Bronze Star Medal based on the award of the Combat Infantryman Badge
- Purple Heart with five Oak-Leaf Clusters (equivalent to six Purple Hearts. His head injury in Salerno was not cited)
- Good Conduct Medal

Shiro "Kash" Kashino, January 19, 1922 to June 11, 1997. Photo courtesy of the Kashino family

- Distinguished Unit Citation Badge
- European-African-Middle Eastern Campaign Medal with Bronze Service Stars for North Apennines, Po Valley, Rhineland, and Rome-Arno Campaigns
- World War II Victory Medal
- Congressional Gold Medal

Silver Star Citation:

SHIRO KASHINO, 39 919 567, S/Sgt, Infantry, 92nd Infantry Division

For gallantry in action, on 14 April 1945, in Italy. Staff Sergeant KASHINO, then private, led a platoon in an attack on an enemy OP location on a hill overlooking Carrara. Leaving one squad to support the assault as a base of fire, Staff Sergeant KASHINO led two squads to the foot of their objective where he sent one squad to the right and one to the left while he proceeded alone to the peak on the reverse slope. Reaching the top, he encountered two enemy emplacements, each manned by two enemy soldiers. Opening up with this submachine gun, he killed two and wounded a third as he fled down the slope of the hill. Meanwhile, hostile forces began firing on the assault group from three sides and the platoon leader asked for volunteers to go back and ask for mortar support. He volunteered to go and, while descending the hill, noticed a number of his men who were wounded and under enemy gunfire. The foe fired at him but he delivered his message to the mortar section and returned to aid the wounded, found their strength depleted by casualties, and went back to the mortar section and obtained makeshift litters and bearers who, directed by him, evacuated the injured. He then returned to the top of the hill and reorganized his men for a defense. At dawn, the foe counterattacked again but Staff Sergeant KASHINO fully exposed himself and wounded 2 and pinned down 3 more of the foe who were attempting to creep up on his position. His heroic gallantry exemplified the highest traditions of the American soldier.

GO No. 100
Hq 92nd Inf Div,
20 Oct 45

Award of Bronze Star Medal:

By direction of the President, under the provisions of Army Regulations 600-45, 22 September 1943, as amended, the Bronze Star Medal is awarded by the Army Group Commander to the following named individuals:

1 April 45

SHIRO KASHINO, 39919567, Staff Sergeant, Inf., Company "I", *** Regimental Combat Team, for heroic achievement on 27 October 1944 in the vicinity of La Houssiere, France. When his company's forward elements were pinned down by machine gun fire from high ground and the company's left flank exposed due to the withdrawal of supporting elements, Sergeant Kashino, exposing himself to enemy observation, dashed 50 yards up a hill. Shouting to his comrades to follow he covered their advance and organized a firing line. From this point he directed fire which neutralized the machine gun position and enabled the forward elements of his company to withdraw to higher ground. Sergeant Kashino was the last to leave, covering his men's withdraw with his submachine gun.

From:
DEPARTMENT OF THE ARMY
OFFICE OF THE ADJUTANT GENERAL
U.S. ARMY ADMINISTRATION CENTER
ST. LOUIS, MISSOURI 63132

Kash's greatest strength in caring for his men and his having little use for authority may have resulted in retaliation from the battalion commander, Lt. Col. Pursell. Many of the men of the 442nd believed that Kash's court-martial would never have happened had his relations with Lt. Colonel Pursell been better, as it was convened by Pursell himself. But despite that, the men of the 442nd remembered Kash as a fearless "soldier's soldier," and a true leader who never asked his men to do anything he wasn't willing to do himself. Tragically, despite his gallantry and heroism in World War II, it wasn't until after his death in 1997 that the disgrace and his conviction for a crime he did not commit was overturned by the Judge Advocate General of the United States Army.

For his gallantry during the battle of the Gothic Line, Kash was recommended for the Distinguished Service Cross, the Army's second-highest medal behind the Medal of Honor. But when Shiro was (wrongly) court-martialed and convicted, the Army instead awarded him the Silver Star. Lt. Colonel Mark Harvey, who reviewed Kash's appeal decades later said "Still, he was awarded the Silver Star after he was arrested. That's pretty impressive."

Note: It is this author's hope that the recommendation for Kash's Silver Star to be upgraded to the Distinguished Service Cross will someday be posthumously awarded and upgraded to the Congressional Medal of Honor since his court-martial conviction was later overturned.

"If not for the unjustified court martial, Kash would have been at least a Lieutenant, and should have gotten the Distinguished Service Cross."
—Fred Matsumura

"Kash should have gotten the Medal of Honor, not me. He was a soldier's soldier."
—Barney Hajiro

He was one of the most highly decorated American soldiers of World War II and was highly respected by the men of the 442nd and all who knew him. But as much as he was honored for his gallantry during the war, his greatest love and loyalty was with his family and the Japanese American community.

While he had the option of being buried in the Veterans Memorial area of the Evergreen Washelli Cemetery in Seattle, Washington, he opted to be buried in the Japanese American area instead. His marker reads Shiro Kashino, KASH, Staff Sergeant, U.S. Army.

And he shall be honored forevermore as Staff Sergeant Shiro "KASH" Kashino.

"We were fortunate to have made a name for ourselves . . . 442nd could have been a bunch of cowards. We could have run away . . . We could have made a lousy name for ourselves... But we fought to prove our loyalty . . . and we did pretty good."

—Shiro "Kash" Kashino

EPILOGUE

American Grit

What is American Grit? The generation of Americans born between 1901 and 1927 is popularly known as the "Greatest Generation." According to the website Investopedia, they are Americans who lived through the economic hardships of the Great Depression and wartime hardships of World War II, and are generally characterized as patriotic, driven, motivated, hard-working, prudent savers, committed, and loyal.

Most modern definitions of "grit" include perseverance, passion, and hard work to achieve long term goals. To me, American Grit is special. It goes beyond just "grit." It is uniquely about the ideals of America, and having the vision, passion, perseverance, and courage to work hard and fight for something greater than yourself for the greater good. It is this author's view that those Americans of the Greatest Generation personified American Grit as they fought through the Great Depression and World War II, then went on to build one of the most prosperous eras in American history.

While it is impossible to share all the incredible stories of American Grit that happened during and after World War II, the experiences shared in this book exemplify what I believe American Grit to be and am honored to share some of them with you.

American Grit: Shiro "Kash" Kashino

Kash's entire life was about taking care of others and making life better for his family, community, and country, and always fought for what he thought was right. His life's mission was to make life better for Japanese Americans by proving his loyalty and patriotism, and he became one of the most decorated American soldiers in World War II after having volunteered from a Japanese American concentration camp. He went on to live an honorable life and died an American hero.

American Grit: Louise Kashino

Louise was a remarkable woman who never gave up on Kash, or her hope for Japanese Americans to live in freedom, and always remained faithful to her family and country. Despite feeling as if America abandoned them during World War II, she believed that America was worth fighting for. She knew Japanese Americans to be good people, and never gave up on winning the hearts and minds of America and worked hard as an honest, law-abiding citizen for her entire life.

In many ways, Louise personified the old saying that *"Behind every great man stands an even greater woman."* When asking Louise about how she felt about the hardships and injustices she faced with Executive Order 9066 and what she had to go through to get Kash's rank of staff sergeant reinstated and his court-martial overturned, Louise replied 'Isn't it wonderful that we live in a country where they made a mistake and admitted it, and righted a wrong? We're lucky that we live in this country."

Louise did not have the medals or accolades to her name that Kash had, but in her own quiet way, she too proved her loyalty to the United States, and will also be remembered as an American hero.

American Grit: 100th Infantry Battalion and 442nd Regimental Combat Team

One of the greatest challenges in writing this book was the realization that every 100th/442nd veteran and survivor of Minidoka I interviewed had their own incredible experiences from World War II. While I focused on Kash and Louise Kashino and a few others in this book, my greatest regret is that I could not include all of their stories.

With their motto, "Go for Broke," meaning to put everything on the line to win big, the Japanese American men of the 100th/442nd started with tremendous disadvantages, including their physical stature being three inches shorter and twenty pounds lighter than the average American infantry soldier. But what they lacked in physical size they more than made up for with an indomitable spirit to prove their loyalty and patriotism.

While many of the men felt like the Army viewed them as expendable "cannon fodder," the fact of the matter was that the 100th/442nd became known as a regiment that won battles when nobody else could. As such, military commanders called on them to succeed when all else failed. As Kash would later recall, he and others considered it as more of an opportunity for them to make a name for themselves and prove their loyalty to the United States of America. According to Arlington National Cemetery: *In total, 650 men of the 100th/442nd were killed in action with 9,486 casualties.*

Today, the 442nd Regimental Combat Team, including the 100th Battalion, has the distinction of being the most decorated fighting unit for its size and length of service in the history of the United States Military. The National Museum of War confirms that this unit was awarded:

- 7 Presidential Distinguished Unit Citations (Equivalent to a Distinguished Service Cross for the unit)

EPILOGUE: AMERICAN GRIT

- 2 Meritorious Service Unit Commendations
- 1 Congressional Gold Medal
- 21 Medals of Honor
- 29 Distinguished Service Crosses
- 560 Silver Stars (Gallantry in action)
- 28 Silver Stars with Oak Leaf Clusters (In lieu of second award)
- 36 Army Commendations
- 87 Division Commendations
- 18 Decorations from Allied Nations
- 9,486 Purple Hearts (For wounds or deaths in action)
- 22 Legions of Merit (Exceptional meritorious services)
- 15 Soldier's Medals (non-combat heroism)
- 4,000+ Bronze Stars (heroic or meritorious achievement)
- 1,200 Bronze Stars with Oak Leaf Cluster

Note: These are the combined counts of awards, honors, and statistics for the 442nd RCT, including the 100th Battalion.

On July 15, 1946, survivors of the 442nd marched down Constitution Avenue in Washington, D.C., becoming the first military unit returning from the war to be reviewed by President Harry S. Truman.

President Harry S. Truman presents a Presidential Unit Citation to the 442nd RCT. In his final speech to the 442nd, he said "You fought not only the enemy, but you fought prejudice and you have won. Keep up that fight, and we'll continue to win." Photo courtesy of the National Archives and Records Administration

American Grit: The Military Intelligence Service

Over 6,000 Japanese American Nisei men served in the United States Military Intelligence Service (MIS) as America's secret weapon in the war against Japan. As code breakers, interpreters, negotiators, and interrogators, these brave men faced similar racism and discrimination as the Japanese American men of the 100th/442nd did in Europe, with the added danger of looking like the Japanese enemy. According to John Aiso, an MIS veteran, "We may have been the only soldiers in history to have bodyguards to protect us from our own forces in combat zones so we would not be mistaken for the enemy."

As well, the Japanese American men of the MIS were well aware that the Imperial Japanese Armed Forces considered them to be Japanese nationals, and that their capture would have resulted in their execution as traitors. Major General Charles Willoughby, General

MacArthur's Chief of Intelligence in the Pacific, credited the MIS with shortening the war with Japan and saving a million lives. The Japanese Americans who served during World War II in the Military Intelligence Service, the 100th Infantry Battalion, and the 442nd Regimental Combat Team were collectively presented the Congressional Gold Medal on November 2, 2011, over sixty-six years after the end of World War II.

American Grit: Inmates of the Japanese American Concentration Camps

They were jailed for their heritage. They lost their homes, businesses, and land. They had no idea what their future held. They were reviled, hated, and distrusted by their fellow citizens. They were evicted from their homes and imprisoned in desolate internment camps, and yet every one of them believed in the American ideal of freedom and opportunity. In their own way, they fought for what they thought was right *as Americans*. They fought for their constitutional rights and to prove their loyalty. From Minidoka alone, over 1,000 men went to war for the United States. Seventy-three died in combat, and many of their parents were presented a Gold Star with an American flag by American Army officers while they were prisoners of the United States Army. But still they fought for their future. Still, they held their dreams of freedom. While 193 internees died at Minidoka, over 1,000 children were born there. Then they were evicted from their prison homes and given $25 and a one-way ticket to somewhere, anywhere, rendering many of them homeless and on their own to start a new life.

The Japanese American inmates of Minidoka and all of the ten internment camps believed in America. They believed in their dreams of freedom. They believed in justice. They believed in themselves as Americans. They fought for it all and persevered through the greatest of hardships . . . and they won.

American Grit: The No-No Boys

The No-No Boys believed their cause of fighting for the Constitutional rights of Japanese Americans to be as righteous and justified as any other. Those who refused the (eventual) draft were given three-year sentences in maximum security federal prisons and were characterized as disloyal cowards, with Japanese American communities blaming them for the American public's perception of Japanese Americans being unpatriotic.

While their actions were considered by many to be counterproductive to proving the loyalty and patriotism of Japanese Americans, courage comes in different forms and their efforts would be vindicated decades later with the rise of the civil rights movement.

Today they are considered heroes in their own right for having stood up against the injustices of Executive Order 9066.

American Grit: Pastor Emery "Andy" Andrews and his family. Courage under fire.

Despite knowing the hardships he and his family would suffer in the face of racism and being labeled a "Jap Lover," Andy moved his family to Twin Falls, Idaho, to support the Japanese internees both personally and spiritually. He would often receive requests for belongings left in the church gymnasium to be delivered to their owners in Minidoka. In total, he made more than thirty trips and drove over 42,000 miles between Seattle and Minidoka as he braved the rugged desert and mountain roads, rain, snow, and desert heat in his old Chevy truck he converted into a bus.

At the end of the war, when many returning Japanese internees found their belongings to have been lost, stolen, or sold, Andy and the Japanese Baptist Church made sure that 100 percent of the belongings left and trusted to them were returned to their owners. Andy always encouraged people to do what was right despite the opposing hardships they might face, and supported civil rights before it became a national priority. After he left the Baptist Church, Kash and Dr. Uyeno enlisted the help of the Nisei Veteran's Club to help pay for some of Andy's living expenses out of gratitude for all he did for the Japanese American community. They felt it was the least they could do to help the man that had done so much for them. When Andy passed away in 1976, over 1,000 people attended his funeral, the highest attendance of any event in the history of the Japanese Baptist Church.

It also bears noting that there were many people who did good things for the Japanese internees including caring for their belongings and properties, supporting them whenever they could, and being there for them when they returned from Minidoka to restart their lives. All of them challenged the belief that "They look like the enemy so they must be the enemy," and fought the tide of fear and racism despite accusations of being "Jap Lovers."

To all those who supported the Japanese American community at their time of greatest need, thank you, and God bless you.

American Grit: The United States Government

In 1983, the federal Commission on Wartime Relocation and Internment of Civilians estimated the economic losses of Japanese Americans interned during World War II to be as high as $6.2 billion (which in 2023 terms would approximate $19 billion). President Ronald Reagan signed the Civil Liberties Act in 1988, providing a formal apology and $20,000 to the living Japanese Americans who were incarcerated during World War II. While Kash, Louise, and Japanese Americans across the country were pleased, it wasn't the money that was the main cause for celebration. Rather, they were elated with the acknowledgment by the Congress and President of the United States that a wrong had been committed and action was being taken on behalf of those directly affected. In the words of President Reagan in 1988: "No payment can make up for those lost years. So what is most important in this bill has less to do with property than with honor. For here we admit a wrong: here we reaffirm our commitment as a nation to equal justice under the law."

American Grit: You and me

The stories of the Japanese American internment/concentration camps and the 442nd Regimental Combat Team during World War II are fading from the American identity. As important moments in the history of America that are not being widely taught, they are at risk of being forgotten and cancelled. History forgotten will inevitably be repeated, and history canceled becomes history forgotten.

Despite the best of intentions, it is possible—if not likely—that another event will happen that will cause fear and hysteria to spread across the country. Remember 9/11. As the entire country galvanized around the destruction of the World Trade Center, there were many who called for arresting and detaining all Muslims, simply because they were Muslims. Fortunately, calmer heads prevailed, with many refusing to repeat the experience of the Japanese American internment camps of World War II.

While we have made tremendous progress in civil rights since World War II, our country and the ideal of equal justice under the law continues to be under attack. Where we once celebrated debate and tolerance, we now impose institutional ideologies on one another. It was the Kashino's great wish that the experience of Japanese Americans and valor of the 442nd RCT during World War II never be forgotten and that we make every effort to educate ourselves and the public of the tragedy of Executive Order 9066 to ensure that our Constitutional right to equal justice under the law is afforded to every citizen of the United States of America.

Let us never forget.

My American Grit Journey—John J. Suzuki

American Grit is the story of a miracle that became a mission of love. My journey started in 2008, when I visited my mom at her Japanese assisted living home in Seattle. As I took the elevator to her floor, I saw a flyer about a three-day pilgrimage to a place called Minidoka happening two months later. Since I didn't know much about what a "pilgrimage" was, I just ignored it as I do the thousands of ads I see every day.

In the following weeks, I was surprised to see that Minidoka flyer just about everywhere I went—in grocery stores, restaurants, and even a college ten miles outside of Seattle—and I started to get the creepy feeling that it was following me. Finally, I decided that I shouldn't ignore it anymore when I found a Minidoka flyer on my windshield the day before the pilgrimage. It was weird. Then, when I called the phone number to see if there were any openings for me to participate, I was told "this must be your lucky day," as someone had canceled just minutes prior to my call. It was clear to me that I was supposed to be on this trip.

As a third generation Japanese American (Sansei) and son of an American Nisei veteran of World War II myself, I have always had an inherent interest in the Japanese American concentration camps. Although neither of my parents was directly affected since my dad lived outside the military exclusion zone and my mom lived in Kuwana, a small town in Mie Prefecture in Japan, the internment camps had to do with my own heritage and freedoms as a Japanese American. And having grown up in Los Angeles, I was well aware of the camp experiences suffered by so many of my friends' parents. But because the pilgrimage to Minidoka was at a time in my life when I had a growing family to care for and a career that required sixty-hour work weeks and traveling two to three weeks a month, taking three days out of my life was a really big deal. As such, it was with a tremendous sense of anticipation and curiosity that I boarded the bus the next day.

On the twelve-hour bus ride to Twin Falls, Idaho, everyone on the bus introduced themselves and shared their reasons for joining the pilgrimage to Minidoka. I was the only person on the pilgrimage whose family did not have any connection to having been imprisoned there during World War II. I explained that I truly had no idea why I was going, but fully expected that the reason would be revealed to me by the time we got on the bus home.

The days that followed were some of the most sobering and humbling days of my life. To see and imagine the conditions that the Japanese American prisoners of Minidoka had to endure made me wonder how my country, the United States of America, could subject its own citizens to such cruelty for no other reason than their heritage. The stories and experiences shared by folks who had their life's hard work and possessions stolen, sold, or lost were nothing less than heartbreaking. Others spoke of the hardships and brutality of desert life and losing loved ones who died while imprisoned in Minidoka. But as heart wrenching as the first day was, I went to bed with my purpose for being there still a mystery. Perhaps I missed it, or perhaps the morning's Minidoka remembrance ceremony would offer some clues.

The next morning, we arrived at Minidoka and stood in front of a kind of billboard called the "Honor Roll," which listed the names of the inmates of Minidoka who had volunteered to fight in the United States Army during World War II. I could not believe it. Who in their right mind would willingly fight and die for the U.S. Army when it was the U.S. Army that imprisoned them and their families in Minidoka in the first place? And then it hit me: the purpose for my being there was to learn about this and share the story of the Japanese American internment camps, and the men who volunteered from those camps to fight and die for America. It was an unbelievable story and one that had to be shared with the world.

As the son of a Japanese American veteran of World War II, I was familiar with the 442nd RCT. My father was part of the Military

Intelligence Service (MIS), a top-secret group of second-generation Japanese Americans tasked with interpreting and decoding Japanese communications and interrogating Japanese prisoners of war. Their efforts were credited with accelerating the end of the war with Japan and saving over one million lives. But because much of the work of the MIS remained classified for decades after the war, there were few stories that made the headlines compared to that of the 442nd, whose courage and battle record were deservedly legendary. So, as I thought of the storyline of what I first imagined as a screenplay for a major motion picture, I focused my attention on finding a man who was interred in Minidoka, volunteered for the U.S. Army's 442nd Regimental Combat team to prove his loyalty, and fought in two of the most famous and celebrated battles in U.S. Military history: The battles of the Lost Battalion and Gothic Line.

Finding Kash

After weeks of research, I came across a man named Shiro Kashino, and thus began my journey in writing this book. It took several days to get over my disappointment in learning that he had died in 1997, but I resolved to finish this project no matter what. After all, I grew up with my mom teaching me the Japanese proverb "Nanakorobi yaoki," which means to fall down seven times and get up eight.

My next hope was to connect with Kash's widow, Louise. Figuring that she lived on the West Coast, I combed through as many phone books as I could find. Unfortunately, of the seventeen Kashinos I found in Washington, Oregon, and California, none of them were Louise. So, I decided to send registered letters introducing myself as an aspiring screenwriter hoping to meet with Louise Kashino to discuss the project I was contemplating. After all, one of them had to know her, right? After several weeks went by with no answer, I again sent the seventeen registered letters hoping to connect with Louise, realizing that the odds of my letter reaching her were slim to none.

On top of that, the chances of Louise agreeing to meet with me, a complete stranger who for all she knew could be an axe murderer, were not very promising.

It's Her!

I was on a business trip in Nags Head, a town in the Outer Banks of North Carolina, when my cell phone rang and the woman on the other end introduced herself as Louise Kashino responding to my letter. It was a day and a moment in my life I will never forget. I was with a colleague of mine, Bryan Boice, who I had told about my hope to connect with Louise. Excited out of my mind, I motioned to Bryan "IT'S HER! IT'S HER!"

Louise explained that her daughter, Debbie Kashino, had received one of my registered letters. After telling her about my interest in her and her late husband's life story, she agreed to meet with my wife and me for breakfast when I returned to Seattle. Thus began my incredible relationship with one of the most magnificent women I have ever met.

I learned that Louise had spent her entire career as a legal secretary, and I realized instantly that she must have been an extraordinary one. She had more information and resources on Kash, his comrades, and his World War II experiences than I could have ever hoped for, and everything was meticulously organized. She also had the names and contact information of all the people I wanted to meet—and many more—including Barney Hajiro and U.S. Senator Daniel Inouye, who were Congressional Medal of Honor (MOH) recipients of the 442nd Regimental Combat Team.

The Incredibles

In November of 2009, Louise gave me the honor of attending the sixty-fifth anniversary celebration of the Rescue of the Lost Battalion in Texas that included rescuing members of the 442nd RCT. It was there that I met Mutt Sakumoto, the first infantryman of the 442nd to reach the Lost Battalion who's famous first words were "You want a cigarette?"

I also met Kenneth Inada, who was one of the surviving men who volunteered for the supply detail with Kash on the ill-fated supply run ordered by Lt. Colonel Pursell during the Battle of the Lost Battalion. He was severely injured in the leg and recalled Kash carrying him to safety and saving his life. I also had the honor of meeting The Honorable Norman Mineta, MOH recipient George Sakato, Lawson Sakai, and Susumu Ito, who famously carried a camera with him against regulations throughout World War II and photographed many of his experiences with the 442nd. While the men I met have since passed away, I will never forget their kindness and humility in welcoming me into their family.

Daniel Inouye, 442nd RTC, Medal of Honor Recipient and United States Senator

Later in December of 2009, Louise arranged for me to meet with United States Senator Daniel Inouye in his chambers in Washington, DC. Senator Inouye was the Chairman of the powerful Senate Appropriations Committee and a very busy man. It was only because of Louise's request that he granted me a twenty-minute personal audience. Senator Inouye was a complete gentleman and shared stories of his own World War II experience; how he lost his arm in the Battle of the Gothic Line, and his actions that earned him the Congressional Medal of Honor.

After recovering from his severe injuries from the Battle of the Gothic Line, 2nd Lt. Daniel Inouye was shipped home to the United States. While his right arm had to be amputated, he was happy to have survived the war when so many of his comrades were left behind in cemeteries in Europe. As a war hero, Inouye served the United States Army with honor, and kept his promise of never bringing shame to his family or his country.

Upon his arrival back in the States, he stepped into a barber shop wearing his American Army uniform—and missing an arm—and was greeted by the barber who told him to read the sign that said, "We don't cut Jap hair." After all he did to serve his country and that barber, he realized that the prejudice against him and other Japanese Americans would continue despite his heroism and service to his country. He was later scheduled to travel back to his home in Hawaii via California, but at the last minute, Inouye was bumped from the flight to California and placed on a later flight. When he arrived in California, he learned that the plane he got bumped from went down and all aboard perished. On his long flight from California to Hawaii, Inouye recalled his trip home:

> *I was sitting in the back of the plane when a full bird colonel walked back from the front and asked if I was with the 442nd. When I told him yes, he said that the general at the front of the plane wanted to see me. I asked the colonel why, and the colonel just said that if a general wants to see me, that I should probably go see him. So the colonel took my seat at the back of the plane, and I went up front to see the general. As I was walking up, I was worried that I was in trouble. After I saluted the general, he asked me if I was with the 442nd and I said, 'yes sir.' He then thanked me for my service and shook my hand. As I started to head back to my seat in the back of the plane, the general told me to sit down next to him for the rest of the flight. When I asked him about the colonel, he told me not to worry about him. I flew all the way to Hawaii in the front of the plane with the general, and I'm sure the colonel was not happy with me at all. It was a really long flight in that two-prop plane.*
>
> *When we landed on Oahu, the general asked me how I was getting home. I told him that I was just going to walk to a pay phone and call a cab, but the general insisted that his driver take me home. When I asked the general how he was going to get home he said,*

'Son, in this United States Army you don't worry about generals.' And then he went on to give me instructions. He told me to call my mom from a pay phone a few blocks from my house and let her know that I'm coming home and to come out front. Then when the driver pulled up to the house, I was to make sure my mom came outside, and I was to wait until the driver walked around to my door and opened the door for me. Then when I got out, I was to salute the driver, and say 'you're dismissed.' The driver would then salute me and drive off. When I asked the general why, he said that 'showing your mom the respect and admiration the United States Army has for her son is the least we can do to honor her.' I never forgot that. It was quite the homecoming for me.

Daniel Inouye would be promoted to Captain before leaving the Army, and went on to a distinguished career in politics, being the first Hawaiian representative for Hawaii's territorial House of Representatives, and later becoming the first United States Senator when Hawaii became a state in 1960. His Distinguished Service Cross was upgraded to a Congressional Medal of Honor in 2000, and he served as U.S. Senator for the state of Hawaii until his death in 2012, after which he posthumously received the Presidential Medal of Freedom.

Daniel Inouye often spoke of the men of the 442nd who volunteered out of the Japanese American internment camps. *"To this day when I ask myself what I would have done*

United States Senator Daniel Inouye 1924 — 2012. A true American patriot. Photo courtesy of the National Archives and Records Administration.

if I were them, I honestly don't know if I would have volunteered like those guys did, or if I would have just said 'Nuts to you.'"

Barney Hajiro, 442 RCT Medal of Honor Recipient

As I continued my journey in doing my research and meeting with as many people as possible, I asked Louise for an introduction to Barney Hajiro, the SNAFU who had promised Kash that he really wasn't a bad guy and went on to be awarded the MOH for his valor in the Battle of the Lost Battalion. Louise made the arrangements, and I flew to Hawaii to meet Mr. Hajiro and his son at his assisted living home in Honolulu. As I sat in his room with him, all I could think of was the honor of being in the presence of yet another giant of American military history. He was a quiet and humble man, who kept repeating two things as we talked: "Kash was a soldier's soldier," and that Kash deserved the Congressional Medal of Honor more than he did. It was clear to me that his love and respect for Kash would stay in Mr. Hajiro's heart forever. Kash was truly Mr. Hajiro's hero. A hero's hero.

Who is George Morihiro?

George Morihiro was the 442nd soldier who was told by Kash to go out and enjoy himself since they "could be dead tomorrow" on Valentine's Day, 1945, the fateful night of the bar incident in Beausoleil, France. I wanted desperately to interview Mr. Morihiro, but I could not find him. Then one day, my son Michael and I went to visit my mom in her assisted living home in Seattle. As we went into the elevator, Michael pushed the elevator button, and we went to her room. Oddly, the door wouldn't open with my key, and then I got worried when mom didn't answer my knocks on her door. Then came the words that will haunt me forever when Michael asked, "Hey dad, who's George Morihiro?" I had never spoken of Mr. Morihiro to Michael, so a bit bewildered I asked him "How do you know about George Morihiro?"

Then he said, "His name is right here on the door."

Sure enough, the name plate on the door said "George Morihiro." As it turned out, when we entered the elevator, Michael mistakenly hit the second-floor button, when my mom actually lived on the third floor in room 304. As I stood stunned in front of room 204, Mr. Morihiro's room, I realized that he was living in the room directly below my mom's. After weeks of searching for him, we found him ten feet below my mom's room all along!

Up until that moment, mine was truly a journey of miracles; of learning about Minidoka, of being accepted into Louise's life, and doors opening that allowed me to meet legend after legend as I crisscrossed the country. But it was at that moment, standing in front of Mr. Morihiro's room, that I realized something bigger was at play. From that moment on, writing this book became a mission of love.

When I finally met with Mr. Morihiro, he gladly shared stories about how Kash was the best and most courageous man he had ever worked for, and how Kash never retreated, never lost a battle, and never left a man behind. It was clear that he respected and revered Kash, and truly missed him. As we were wrapping up our conversation, he asked if he could give me one piece of advice. As I sat there in rapt attention expecting perhaps the greatest advice ever given, he rolled up his sleeves and said, "Don't you ever get a tattoo."

He went on to say that the tattoo on his arm seemed like a good idea at the time, but over the years, it became nothing but a big smudge. He laughed out loud and said, "Now I have to look at that stupid thing every single day!"

What an honor it was to meet him.

Blocked

As I continued with my research in 2010, I suddenly came to a major roadblock as I found myself unable to muster up the energy or inspiration to continue. It was an incredibly frustrating time for me, especially knowing that this truly was a mission of love that I had to complete. After months of unsuccessfully trying to break through, I decided to put it on the backburner and go with the flow.

It was about eight years later that my daughter Kristin encouraged me to restart my work, and it was then that I learned how truly wise my little girl was. As we analyzed my writer's block, I realized that what was holding me back was my fear of failing. This project, after all, was really a big deal and came with the tremendous responsibility I placed on myself of educating the world so the tragedy of the Japanese American experience of World War II would never be repeated. What if I failed? What if I produced a piece of junk? What if, what if, what if. I was paralyzed. And then Kristin destroyed my writer's block with these words: "Dad, just finish your work and give it to the universe to decide."

It was time to get back to work.

Back to Work

With a great deal of trepidation and anticipation, I called Louise and Debbie and asked if they would be willing to restart the project

John Suzuki, Debbie Kashino, and Louise Kashino
in June, 2019 in Leschi on Lake Washington.

with me. To my great relief and delight, they were both happy to hear from me and were also happy to help me move forward.

The next person Louise encouraged me to meet was Vince Matsudaira, who was a dear friend of hers. The Matsudaira family had been interred at Minidoka, and Vince had spent decades chronicling camp experience and the 442nd, and produced a documentary on Kash's life called *KASH: The Legend and Legacy of Kash Kashino*. Vince offered to help me on my journey and I gladly accepted. It was during a meeting with him that I decided that the next step on my journey was to visit the battlefields of the Lost Battalion in France and Gothic Line in Italy.

Going back to Louise, I asked if she happened to know anyone who could host me for tours of the battlefields in France and Italy, and of course, she did. Louise introduced me to Brian Yamamoto, who was very familiar with historians in Europe who had intimate knowledge of both battles. He graciously gave me the contact information of Gerome Villain in Bruyeres, France, and Davide Del Giudice of Massa, Italy. Shortly thereafter, I found myself on a plane to Europe to visit the now sacred battlegrounds of the Vosges Forest in France and Apennine Mountains of Italy.

Landing in Geneva, Switzerland, my first stop was Lake Annecy in France, where I met up with some dear friends of mine from San Diego who invited me to paraglide with them in the French Alps. Since Lake Annecy happens to be about halfway between Bruyeres and Massa, I used Lake Annecy as my base, which had the added benefit of being a mecca of paragliding.

The Battlegrounds of the Lost Battalion

I headed first to France to meet with Gerome Villain, who took me through the town of Bruyeres, which was liberated by the 442nd from the Germans just before the battle of the Lost Battalion. As we were walking along the road, I mentioned to Gerome that it seemed like a lot of folks were looking at me, and he said, "Of course they are. Everyone thinks you're with the 442nd and are happy you're here!"

It was amazing. More than seven decades later, the people of Bruyeres still honored the men of the 442nd.

John Suzuki and Gerome Villain in Bruyeres, France in 2019. Note the street sign. Translated: "Street of the 442nd American Infantry Regiment, Liberator of Bruyeres, October 1944."

Gerome was very knowledgeable of the Vosges Forest and where the Battle of the Lost Battalion occurred. My first observation was the dense brush (that the Germans used as cover) and the absence of large older trees, since most of them were destroyed by tree bursts during the battle. Now the area was full of smaller trees that had grown since then. Walking through the forest, we found remnants of the battle; shell casings, shrapnel, and bullets that had lain there since 1945. As we went to the area known as "Suicide Hill," Gerome showed me the German placements and the steepness of the terrain where the Germans held the high ground. I imagined how advantaged the Germans were as they lobbed grenades atop the men of the 442nd below them, who had to fight uphill at forty-five-degree inclines in some places. As I explored one of the German foxholes, I suddenly dropped to my knees and cried uncontrollably. Around me I felt the strong and undeniable presence of the men who fought there, and I knew they were there to help me on my journey. I still get goosebumps thinking about that moment. It is truly a sacred place.

As we continued through the forest, Gerome showed me where the Lost Battalion dug in for the siege against the Germans, who had surrounded and isolated them. It was unbelievable to me how unprotected they were as they fought for their lives until they were rescued by the 442nd. Now I could understand the miracle of their survival, and how the men of the Lost Battalion and the 442nd experienced hell on earth.

The Battlegrounds of the Gothic Line

Like Gerome Villain, Davide Del Giudice was the perfect host. Meeting Davide was like meeting a living encyclopedia on the Battle of the Gothic Line. We set off in the morning to Monte Folgorito, which is a mountain peak that serves as the western bookend of the Apennine Mountain range known as the Gothic Line. The morning was cold and foggy, and as we hiked up the road leading up to the Gothic Line—the same road the Germans used when they held the Gothic Line—I wondered if the weather was going to prevent us from seeing anything.

Hiking to the top of Monte Folgorito, we came across a memorial erected in honor of the 442nd about two-thirds of the way up the mountain. Once we reached the top, I was greatly disappointed to see that heavy fog prevented us from seeing anything beyond fifty feet, since I wanted to see what it was like for the German outposts atop the mountains. And then, as if on cue, the fog lifted, giving way to blue skies, and we were suddenly treated to twenty miles of visibility. Again, another miracle.

As we hiked atop the ridges for two miles overlooking the town of Azzano, I was struck by how incredibly narrow and steep the goat trails and ridgetops were. How the 442nd made it all the way up that virtual cliff in the dead of night was beyond my comprehension. As we explored foxholes and bunkers that made the Germans all but immune from Allied attacks, my first observation was how different the battle must have been fighting on the mountaintops compared to the Vosges Forest in France. In this battle, it was clear that speed was key since protective cover was so scarce. As well, since the 442nd secured the top of the ridges first, it was they who were fighting from the high ground this time. I couldn't help but have a tremendous feeling of pride as I imagined the intensity of the battle as the men of the 442nd routed the enemy to accomplish in less than one day what the entire United States 5th Army couldn't accomplish in six months.

As we continued our trek, I came across an old olive tree that Davide and I agreed was probably there at the time of the battle. The tree stood in one of the highest points on the ridge overlooking the area where Kash and I-Company were. Was it possible that Kash came across this tree himself? Maybe the tree protected him. Who knows, right? Knowing that the tree was there when Kash was there made me want to take a piece of it back with me. As I looked around, I found a branch that had broken off that made a perfect walking stick. So, I packed it up, convinced the airline to let me carry it on the plane, and brought it home to Louise along with a picture of the tree. The romantic side of me wants to believe that the tree took care of Kash . . . and the tree was happy.

Writing this book has been one of the greatest pleasures and honors of my life. My research took me from Seattle to Texas, from Hawaii to the halls of Congress, Georgia, France, Italy, Nevada, North Carolina, and many places in between. My hope is that this book will inspire you not only to strive for your own American Grit, but to live your life with it. Live with the courage to fight for what's right and good. Live with the determination and stick-to-itiveness to see things through. My personal belief is that the meaning of life and our reasons for being here are simple: to make the world better than it was when we first got here, and to love one another. And in the final analysis for the "greatest generation" of Japanese Americans who lived through the Great Depression and World War II, they did it all for the sake of the children. That's it. That is American Grit.

God Bless You.

John Suzuki and Davide del Giudice on Monte Folgorito above Massa, Italy in 2019. Note the dates. While the battle raged for over six months, the 442nd ended it in 48 hours.

Acknowledgements

In 2008, Louise Kashino honored me with her permission to share her and her husband's experiences from World War II to educate the world on the tragedy of the Japanese American concentration camps and the heroism of the 442nd Regimental Combat Team. While conflicted with knowing that Mr. Kashino was a humble man and would never have allowed a book like this to be written about him, Louise felt strongly that it was her duty to further the cause of civil rights in America and keep the experience of indiscriminate racism and American concentration camps from ever happening again. Thank you for the honor of sharing your story. And thank you Debbie, Bev, and Kris for supporting my journey.

To Shiro Kashino and all of the men of the 100th Battalion, 442nd RCT, and Military Intelligence Service—including my dad—thank you for your courage, valor, sacrifice, and opening the doors of freedom for me and generations of Americans to come. And to the men of the 442nd I had the honor of interviewing including George Morihiro, Barney Hajiro, Kenneth Inada, Lawson Sakai, George Sakada, Mutt Sakumoto, Susumu "Sus" Ito, and Daniel Inouye, thank you for sharing your stories and experiences with me.

While much of this book was built from interviews, testimonials, and various public records, I wish to give special thanks to Vince Matsudaira for sharing his research behind the making of his outstanding video documentary, *KASH: The Legend and Legacy of Shiro Kashino*. Also special thanks to the Item Chapter of the 442nd Veterans Club in Honolulu for sharing testimonials of the 442nd in the book *And Then There Were Eight*, and Ms. Thelma Chang, author of *I Can Never Forget*. And special thanks to the folks at Densho (Densho.org), for sharing their firsthand recorded testimonials and historical photos of the World War II experience.

Thank you to Gerome Villain for escorting me to the battlefields of the Lost Battalion, and for tolerating the 43°C heat with me (109.4°F), and Davide Del Giudice for taking me to the top of Monte Folgorito and the Gothic Line. Gerome's and Davide's knowledge of the Battles of the Lost Battalion and the Gothic Line was utterly amazing. And to Brian Yamamoto, thank you for introducing me to Gerome and Davide!

To my book coaches, Cristina Smith, Valerie Costa, Christy Day, Maggie McLaughlin, Steve Harrison, Molly Pearson, Steve Scholl, Geoffrey Berwind and Tamara Silberman, this book may have never seen the light of day without you.

And to my dear friends and family who have supported me on this journey as first readers and kept me going; David Eagan, Ken Collins, Bill Furlong, Allison Garr and Sensei Andre' Dulce, Steve and Gail Kaneko, James Fenelon, Craig and Nancy Inouye, Aman Bhutani, David and Adele Fischbach, Lisa Chen, Bryan Boice, John Banczak, Kris Lande, Jules Kirkeby, Kelvin Higa, Les Higa, Flossie and Evan Gull, Jeff Hurst, Mike Zaroudny, Mike and Abbi Suzuki, Kathy Suzuki, and Kristin and David Nguyen, thank you from the bottom of my heart.

And finally, to my far better 99/100, Jeri, thank you for supporting me on this every step of the way. I truly could not have done this without you!

I love you all . . . . John

Resources

Writing this book has been an incredibly special journey and an even more profound honor for me to write. Most of the stories and details I have included in this book have come from testimonies of the actual men and women portrayed in *American Grit*. In addition and of particular note were two books, *And Then There Were Eight — The Men of I Company 442nd Regimental Combat Team* by Item Chapter 442nd Veterans Club, and *I Can Never Forget* by Thelma Chang. Both books offer testimonies on the experiences of 442nd veterans during World War II.

The DVD produced by Mr. Vince Matsudaira titled *KASH: The Legend and Legacy of Shiro Kashino* also includes recorded testimonies of people who knew and fought with Kash and shared their accounts of experiences they shared with him. In addition, Densho (Densho.org) is an invaluable nonprofit organization which documents the testimonies of Japanese Americans who were unjustly incarcerated during World War II, offering irreplaceable firsthand accounts coupled with historical images and teacher resources to explore principles of democracy and promote equal justice for all. Densho is rich in information for anyone wishing to learn more about the Japanese American experience during World War II.

And finally, what makes this book so special is that in addition to including published accounts of the World War II experience, I have included accounts of the war that I have not been able to find referenced in any of my research. For example, Daniel Inouye's account of a 442nd soldier from Seattle motivating the German soldiers from dropping him again as they carried him to the field hospital was something he shared with me personally. As well, while I have not been able to find any official records about Lt. Colonel Pursell's misguided order to retrieve supplies during the Battle of the Lost Battalion that resulted in eight men being killed, my personal interview with Kenneth Inada, who was one of the 442nd volunteers wounded in that supply run and saved by Kash, confirmed that it actually happened.

Finally, Louise Kashino was my greatest source of information, and my greatest cheerleader. For over 40 years, Louise worked as a legal secretary and had very strong organizational and communication skills. She was a meticulous organizer who tracked and remembered everything and was truly remarkable that way. It was through Louise that I met so many incredible people and learned about things that have never been published. From providing letters Kash wrote to her during World War II, to arranging meetings with 442nd Regimental Combat Team members including U.S. Senator and Medal of Honor Recipient (MOH) Daniel Inouye, MOH Recipient Barney Hajiro, MOH recipient George Sakato, Susumu (Sus) Ito, and so many others, to providing contacts for my trips to the battlefields of France and Italy, she was an invaluable guide on my journey in writing this book. She was truly an amazing woman.

Appendix A: A Truly Great Nation

I received approximately a dozen medals, but not because of heroics. In the heat of battle you are not looking for medals. You are simply putting your whole life into fighting for your country. Looking back, we realized how unjust America had been in the way it dealt with its citizens of Japanese ancestry during World War II. Yet I know of no other nation that would openly admit it had been wrong as this nation had done, and then take steps to rectify that wrong. Only a truly great nation dares to make such an admission. This is the America that we fought for and died for.
—Daniel Inouye
442nd RCT, Congressional MOH Recipient, United States Senator

In an era of harsh discrimination against people of Japanese descent, Kash and Louise knew that in order for Japanese Americans to receive acceptance and respect as a race, they first had to do their part to prove they deserved it. For Kash and thousands of other courageous Japanese Americans, World War II was an opportunity to prove their loyalty by fighting America's enemies. Over 1,000 men from Minidoka served in the United States Army. They knew they could die-and seventy-three of them did-but they viewed their sacrifice as the price they had to pay for the freedom of their families, friends, and communities.

Of the more than 122,000 men, women, and children who were imprisoned in American internment camps, not a single one of them, including the No-No Boys, was convicted of crimes against the United

States. In fact, no person of Japanese ancestry in the United States was convicted of espionage or sabotage during the war. By contrast, at least ten white Americans were convicted for spying for Japan.

As American citizens, they suffered unimaginable distress as their Constitutional rights were betrayed; no due process, no equal protection under the law, no rights against unreasonable searches and seizures, no rights to speedy and public trials, and imprisoned for no other reason than their heritage. And through it all, they committed their lives—and those of their families—to live as law-abiding Americans.

In 1976, President Gerald R. Ford officially and finally repealed Executive Order 9066 and used that occasion to express regret for that policy:

> February 19th is the anniversary of a sad day in American history. It was on that date in 1942 . . . that Executive Order 9066 was issued . . . resulting in the uprooting of loyal Americans . . . We now know what we should have known then—not only was that evacuation wrong, but Japanese Americans were and are loyal Americans . . . I call upon the American people to affirm with me this American Promise—that we have learned from the tragedy of that long-ago experience forever to treasure liberty and justice for each individual American and resolve that this kind of action shall never again be repeated.
>
> — President Gerald Ford

Civil Liberties Act of 1988

In 1985, the United States Congress was presented with a redress proposal named H.R. 442 in honor of the Japanese American 442nd Regimental Combat Team, which had emerged as the most decorated combat unit in World War II. After years of Congressional debate, the Civil Liberties Act was finally accepted by the House of Representatives on August 4, 1988. Congress passed the Act to provide a Presidential apology and symbolic payment of $20,000 to surviving American citizens and legal residents of Japanese ancestry who lost liberty or property because of discriminatory action by the Federal government during World War II.

Remarks By President Ronald Reagan on Signing the Bill Providing Restitution for the Wartime Internment of Japanese American Civilians

August 10, 1988

The Members of Congress and distinguished guests, my fellow Americans, we gather here today to right a grave wrong. More than forty years ago, shortly after the bombing of Pearl Harbor, 120,000 persons of Japanese ancestry living in the United States were forcibly removed from their homes and placed in makeshift internment camps. This action was taken without trial, without jury. It was based solely on race, for these 120,000 were Americans of Japanese descent.

Yes, the nation was then at war, struggling for its survival, and it's not for us today to pass judgment upon those who may have made mistakes while engaged in that great struggle. Yet we must recognize that the internment of Japanese Americans was just that: a mistake. For throughout the war, Japanese Americans in the tens of thousands remained utterly loyal to the United States. Indeed, scores of Japanese Americans volunteered for our Armed Forces, many stepping forward in the internment camps themselves. The 442nd Regimental Combat Team, made up entirely of Japanese Americans, served with immense distinction to defend this nation; their nation. Yet back at home, the soldiers' families were being denied the very freedom for which so many of the soldiers themselves were laying down their lives.

Congressman Norman Mineta, with us today, was ten years old when his family was interned. In the Congressman's words: "My own family was sent first to Santa Anita Racetrack. We showered in the horse paddocks. Some families lived in converted stables, others in hastily thrown together barracks. We were then moved to Heart Mountain, Wyoming, where our entire family lived in one small room of a crude tar paper barrack."

Like so many tens of thousands of others, the members of the Mineta family lived in those conditions not for a matter of weeks or months, but for three long years.

The legislation that I am about to sign provides for a restitution payment to each of the 60,000 surviving Japanese Americans of the 120,000 who were relocated or detained. Yet no payment can make up for those lost years. So, what is most important in this bill has less to do with property than with honor. For here we admit a wrong; here we reaffirm our commitment as a nation to equal justice under the law.

I'd like to note that the bill I'm about to sign also provides funds for members of the Aleut community who were evacuated from the Aleutian and Pribilof Islands after a Japanese attack in 1942. This action was taken for the Aleuts' own protection, but property was lost or damaged that has never been replaced.

And now in closing, I wonder whether you'd permit me one personal reminiscence, one prompted by an old newspaper report sent to me by Rose Ochi, a former internee. The clipping comes from the Pacific Citizen and is dated December 1945.

"Arriving by plane from Washington," the article begins, "General Joseph W. Stilwell pinned the Distinguished Service Cross on Mary Masuda in a simple ceremony on the porch of her small frame shack near Talbert, Orange County. She was one of the first Americans of Japanese ancestry to return from relocation centers to California's farmlands."

'Vinegar Joe' Stilwell was there that day to honor Kazuo Masuda, Mary's brother. You see, while Mary and her parents were in an internment camp, Kazuo served as staff sergeant to the 442nd Regimental Combat Team. In one action, Kazuo ordered his men back and advanced through heavy fire, hauling a mortar. For twelve hours, he engaged in a singlehanded barrage of Nazi positions. Several weeks later at Cassino, Kazuo staged another lone advance. This time it cost him his life.

The newspaper clipping notes that her two surviving brothers were with Mary and her parents on the little porch that morning. These two brothers, like the heroic Kazuo, had served in the United States Army. After General Stilwell made the award, the motion picture actress Louise Allbritton, a Texas girl, told how a Texas battalion had been saved by the 442nd. Other show business personalities paid tribute—Robert Young, Will Rogers, Jr., and one young actor who said, "Blood that has soaked into the sands of a beach is all of one color. America stands unique in the world: the only country not founded on race but on a way; an ideal. Not in spite of but because of our polyglot background, we have had all the strength in the world. That is the American way."

The name of that young actor—I hope I pronounce this right—was Ronald Reagan. And, yes, the ideal of liberty and justice for all—that is still the American way.

Thank you, and God bless you. And now let me sign H.R. 442, so fittingly named in honor of the 442nd.

Thank you all again, and God bless you all. I think this is a fine day.

Note: The President spoke at 2:33 p.m. in Room 450 of the Old Executive Office building. H.R 442, approved August 10, was assigned Public Law N. 100—383.

— Ronald Reagan Presidential Library

The Civil Liberties Act of 1988 was the culmination of the recognition of a wrong done, an official apology of the United States government, and vindication of a people so wrongly accused. It was what Kash, Louise, and thousands of others had fought so hard for over more than four decades. The only regret of many was that the people who lost the most had already passed away and were not alive to receive the apology and restitution payment. Nonetheless, the admission of having been so wronged and the recognition of people of Japanese descent being loyal and patriotic American citizens served as the vindication that so many Japanese Americans had fought so hard for since the beginning of World War II.

May we always honor the past by educating the future.

Memorial in honor of the 442nd Regimental Combat Team, 100th Battalion, and Military Intelligence Service at Camp Shelby, Mississippi.

Thank you for reading *American Grit*. If you learned something and enjoyed it, I would be honored with a review on Amazon, if even a sentence or two.

On behalf of all of those represented in *American Grit*, thank you for honoring them and joining me in sharing their story.

God bless you,
John Suzuki

About the Author
www.JohnSuzuki.com

As the host of the highly acclaimed "*Finding Better Podcast*" found on YouTube, Apple, Spotify, and all major podcast platforms, John and his guests share real-life experiences in finding better that his audience can apply to their own lives. In a world that seems so hard and broken, John believes that we all share a common purpose, which is to make the world better than the day we landed on it. "When you lift others, you lift the world, and the best way to lift others is to help them find better for themselves."

As the author of *American Grit*, John's purpose is to educate the world on the concentration camp experiences in America during World War II, and the Japanese American men who volunteered from those camps to fight for the United States Army and went on to become American war heroes. It is the true story of men who refused victimhood and refused to blame others for their circumstances and took responsibility for their own futures and fought for a better world, and they won.